The Author

Lindsay Jenkins has an honours degree in mediaeval and modern history from Bedford College, London University and an MBA from Cranfield School of Management. She spent nearly ten years as a senior civil servant in the Ministry of Defence and another ten years in the City of London working for both British and American investment banks. She is well known in the world markets as a leading forecaster of the international pharmaceutical industry. She now writes full time and lives in both the UK and US.

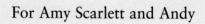

For Amy Scarlett and Andy

THE LAST DAYS OF BRITAIN

The Final Betrayal

LINDSAY JENKINS

Illustrated by Alice Leach

Orange State Press
Washington D.C.

First published in 2001

by Orange State Press
a division of Orange State Communications
PO Box 1132
Palm Beach FL33480
USA
www.orangestatepress.com

UK distributor
The June Press Ltd
PO Box 9984
London W12 8WZ
Telephone and fax: 44+(0)20-8746 1206
www.junepress.com

ISBN 0-9657812-2-4

Phototypeset in 10¼ pt on 13¼ pt Linotron Sabon
by Intype London Ltd

Printed in Great Britain by Biddles Ltd, Guildford

CONTENTS

ACKNOWLEDGEMENTS

I have received valued help from many people and it is invidious to begin a list for fear of having left someone out. There is also a much wider group of people who have been enthusiastic in their support of this project: they are so many that I hope they will accept a general and heartfelt thank you.

I would specifically like to thank:

Christopher Arkell, Tony Bennett, Sir Richard Body MP, Keith Carson of *eurofacts*, Torquil Dick-Erikson, Nigel Farage, Idris Francis, Colin Heaton, Rodney Howlett, Lord Lamont of Lerwick, Ian Milne of *eurofacts*, Richard O'Riordan, Lord Pearson of Rannock, Lee Rotherham, Thomas Russell, Christopher Skeate, Tom Slator, Karen Stevens, Neil and Gillian Turner and once again the outstanding and understanding staff of the London Library.

Alice Leach, with great good humour, has gone far beyond the call of duty. Anthony Martin has again been my salvation with his pithy, detailed and astute comments.

The Foreword
by
Norman Lamont

The Last Days of Britain, The Final Betrayal is a dramatic
title for a book. Is it over done and over dramatic? I don't
think so. In any case, anyone who thinks that should read this
book.

Debate about Britain's place in Europe ever since the war
has been characterised by a lack of candour. Even before the
EEC was created, when the iron and steel communities started continental politicians like Adenauer and Schuman made
it quite clear that the purpose of European integration was in
their word 'federal'. Down the years British ministers of all
persuasions have quibbled over this word. British governments have even been known to plead with the German government not to use the word because it so upset the British.

Most recently, particularly in his speech at Warsaw, the
Prime Minister has sought to argue that federalism is a false
bogy and that his government believes firmly in a 'Europe of
Nation States'. That phrase is marginally better than the so
called 'Europe of Nations', a phrase wrongly ascribed to
General de Gaulle. But it is perfectly possible to have a federation of nation states and indeed revealingly M. Delors has
used that very phrase 'a federation of nation states' to
describe his vision of Europe. The phrase 'Nation State' is
merely a description of where we have come from and what
we have been. In a Federation, a nation state is not necessar-
ily any more powerful that any other type of state. They are
both just components.

Lindsay Jenkins won much praise, and deservedly admiration for her stimulating book *Britain Held Hostage, The Coming Euro-Dictatorship* published in 1997. Now events have moved on, and Britain is further down the road of integration in Europe.

What is particularly alarming is Lindsay Jenkins' account of Europe's attempts to make Europol into a genuinely international police force, and introduce a European prosecutor with tyrannical powers for the pursuit of fraud. All these matters are profoundly far-reaching.

Not everyone will agree with every single part of Lindsay's assessment of where this will lead. No one can deny that it is disturbing. This book is packed with information, and many, not to say chilling, quotations. Like her previous book it is thoroughly research and well sourced.

Lindsay Jenkins is no shrill Europhobe, but a cautious, highly intelligent critic of what is currently happening in Europe. She cuts through much of the verbiage to expose its real nature.

Everyone who cares about the future of this country should read this book.

London
November, 2000

THE RISING TEMPERATURE OF CONTROL

The top priority is to turn the EU into a single political state.

Joshka Fischer, German Foreign Minister in The Times,

26.11.1999

How much authority has Britain already handed over to the European Union in Brussels?

The next two pages are a graphic presentation of the rising temperature of European integration: they illustrate how much power in key areas of government, essential for independence, has already left British shores.

They show the extent of the surrender of British sovereignty and the betrayal of the British people.

As long as the Houses of Parliament remain free, Britain can recover sovereignty by passing an Act of Parliament repealing the European Communities Act (1972).

These estimates were made in October 2000 *before* the impact of the Treaty of Nice.

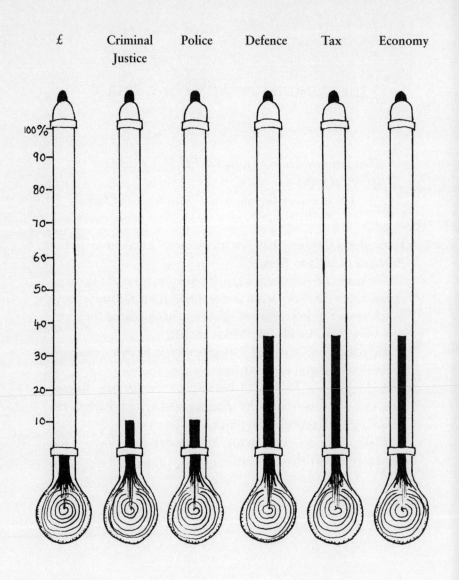

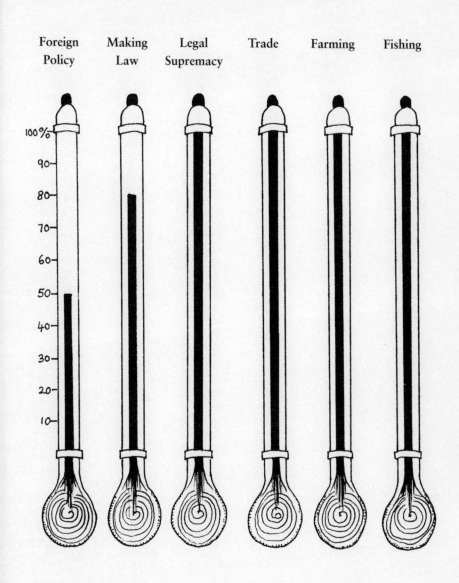

Chapter 1

THE LAST DAYS OF BRITAIN

Today Britain, one of the wealthiest and most successful countries in the world, is approaching its last days as an independent nation. Few in Britain realise how little independence remains, and how most of that remaining freedom could be gone when the Treaty of Nice has been ratified by all 15 EU countries, that is by 2003.

Over the past 40 years, successive British Prime Ministers have knowingly and unknowingly, and little by little, handed control of Britain to a newly emerging superstate, the European Union in Brussels. British governments have routinely pretended that *Brussels'* policies were *British* policies and the British people have been none the wiser.

It is clear that both Conservative and Labour governments have betrayed the people of Britain. The essence of representative government is elections. At no general election have the people of Britain ever been offered a clear choice between a party which favours the end of independence and a party which recognises the reality of the European Union as a dictatorship in the making.

The Franco-German working relationship, which matured as the power behind Brussels, has used every kind of political device to mask the truth and to disguise the reality of creeping *communitisation*: bullying, threatening, harassing, bargaining, horse-trading and bribery.

But Brussels has always been in a position of strength because never once have Britain's leaders seriously considered their *ultimate* option: to regain independence by leaving the European Union. Even in recent years when European politicians have been more open about seeking an integrated and united country called 'Europe', British politicians have been in denial.

The Conservative Party under Edward Heath took Britain into the EEC in 1973. Heath has since admitted that he knew at the time that the EEC planned eventual political union. He failed to tell the people.

Sir Con O'Neill, the British diplomat who led Heath's negotiations, wrote that the government's guiding principle was 'swallow the lot and swallow it now.' The negotiations were secondary. In his report of the talks that was kept secret until September 2000 he recorded,

> 'What mattered was to get into the Community and thereby restore our position at the centre of European affairs which, since 1958, we had lost. None of [the Community's] policies was essential to us; many of them were objectionable. But in order to get in we either had to accept them or to secure agreed adaptations.'
>
> *Britain's Entry into the European Community, 1972*

Even before British entry, Heath agreed with France and Germany to create one currency within a decade. A world oil crisis saved Britain from surrendering the pound.

Only once have the British people been consulted on this process of liquidating their freedom. In 1975 the Labour Prime Minister, Harold Wilson, called a referendum, not honestly to listen to peoples' views, but cynically to heal a rift in his own party. The question was 'do you think the United Kingdom should stay in the European Community (the Common Market)?' The Labour government deceived the people by saying the Common Market was 'all about trade,' and posed no threat whatsoever to Britain's sovereignty and constitution. On that limited basis 76 per cent of voters favoured staying in the Common Market.

Margaret Thatcher failed to understand the European issue until it was too late. She signed the Single European Treaty believing it would promote freer trade. None of her advisers warned her that it gave away even more sovereignty, although some knew. Too late, she rebelled against Brussels in her speech at Bruges in 1988. Her successor, John Major, tried to placate the increasingly sceptical members of his party, while himself believing that Britain's place was within the EU. He signed the Maastricht Treaty giving away yet more powers. His Party's manifesto at the 1992 elections included,

> 'The Conservatives have been the party of Britain in Europe for 30 years . . . We have ensured that Britain is at the heart of Europe; a strong and respected partner . . . The Maastricht Treaty was a success both for Britain and for the rest of Europe. British proposals helped to shape the key provisions of the Treaty including those strengthening the enforcement of Community law, defence, subsidiarity and law and order.'

Under William Hague, the Conservative Party in opposition has markedly increased its scepticism to the point of wanting to keep Britain's currency for one parliament, and to maintain an independent defence under the umbrella of NATO. The Party says it wishes to veto further transfers of power from Westminster to Brussels.

The Conservative Party has so far failed to address in public the issue of how much power Brussels already has. How would Prime Minister Hague make Britain 'the best place in the world to do business,' as he writes in the Tory manifesto

Believing in Britain, when the economy, tax, regulation and trade are already partly or wholly controlled by Brussels? How can the 'crisis in farming and the countryside' be solved when Brussels calls the shots? How can 'our freedom and independence be defended' when the national veto on EU legislation has long gone in so many areas?

Not all Tory politicians have understood that the European Union is not an *à la carte* menu but a *prix fixe*, a dinner dictated by Brussels.

Tony Blair, the Labour Prime Minister, is in the process of deliberately giving away the rest of Britain's sovereignty and independence. His betrayal of the British people is as great as was the betrayal by Edward Heath. He has already signed the Amsterdam Treaty, and with it more national power has gone. He has given up the British right to opt out of the social chapter, and partially given up the Schengen protocol allowing an opt out from ending national border controls. He has signed the Treaty of Nice giving away more power.

Tony Blair's government appears united in wishing to divide Britain into regions of the EU, to abolish the pound, and to hand over the economy, the criminal justice system, and the British armed forces to Brussels control. Blair may hope to keep just enough sovereignty to win one more general election before people realise that Britain has become merely a province of Europe.

Just like Edward Heath, Blair does not openly admit what he is doing. Instead he uses phrases of disguise, such as 'the conditions have not yet been met' when he really means 'the public is not yet ready to accept the truth.'

Why is Blair handing over the rest of Britain's diminished independence? He must see a political advantage. Either he, like Prime Ministers before him, dreams the impossible dream that Britain will gain power by handing over power. Or he hopes one day to become President of the European

Union, a country as large as the United States and which in the eyes of idealists may one day exceed even the power of America.

In his rush to embrace all things European, Blair has ignored the practical results of his policies. The euro, for example, is an efficient pricing mechanism, making it easy to compare the price of goods for sale across Euroland. But it appears doomed to failure as a monetary and fiscal tool. The socialist Euroland economy it represents is growing slowly, is highly regulated, highly taxed, and protectionist. Not surprisingly, the euro lost 25 per cent of its value against the US dollar in the first eighteen months of its existence.

Blair has worked to subsume the British armed forces in a motley European army. Controlled from Brussels with an inadequate budget, the EU army is likely to prove just as sclerotic as the EU economy: under equipped, undermanned and under the control of yet another multinational bureaucracy.

Will the EU army support British interests? It will probably be most active in Eastern Europe and the Balkans next to the EU's (and Germany's) long eastern and southeastern frontiers. The Treaty of Rome Article 11, Title V requires Britain to preserve the EU's external borders. Those land borders are not a major British interest and yet our troops may be asked to put their lives on the line for them.

The nations of Europe are Britain's friends and neighbours with whom relationships should be and normally are excellent. But who would want a neighbour or a friend to come into their home and order how their family should be run? No-one would want that. On the grand scale of Europe, that is exactly what successive British governments have done. They have allowed Britain's friends and neighbours through treaty rights to dismantle over a thousand years of British heritage, traditions and, above all, freedom.

The limited debate on the merits of Britain in the European Union is driven partly by a *bricks and mortar* mentality in which Britain's physical location, close to the Continent of Europe, is considered the key factor even though Britain has been independent of any European empire for a thousand years. Physical location today is almost meaningless for trade. City of London firms have back offices in India, and manufacturing of even bulky items like cars is done thousands of miles from the point of sale. Above all Britain sells worldwide and is not dependent on Europe for survival and prosperity.

One argument for a European state has been keeping the peace. Yet it is NATO which has kept the peace in Europe since 1948, not the EU. The US spends more money on the defence of Europe than do all the EU countries combined. It may be unpalatable to many 'Europeans', but Europe has remained free largely because of the American commitment to defend the continent.

In a world where computers and the Internet empower individuals, government is likely to become smaller and smaller. In such a world, the monolithic EU stands out like a dinosaur doomed to eventual extinction. Britons must reassert their independence before their freedoms are equally, but much more rapidly, extinct. Britons must reverse the final betrayal while they still can.

Chapter 2

LEGISLATION BOLOGNAISE

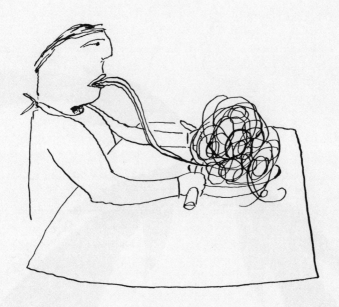

Britain Under Seige

Sovereignty is being eroded and . . . we are coming under another sovereignty – that of Europe . . . the Treaty is like an incoming tide. It flows into the estuaries and up the rivers. It cannot be held back.

Lord Denning, Master of the Rolls, quoted in
Iris Freeman's 'Lord Denning'

Most new *British* law is not British. It comes from the EU in Brussels.

In 1993 about 60 per cent of all legislation going through the British Parliament came from Brussels and was rubber-stamped in London, according to the Hansard Society which promotes more effective parliamentary democracy. The Hansard Society reported that,

> 'Parliament has little if any impact upon the process of European law making. Where successful changes are introduced from the UK, these are usually done by various interested sectors and bodies. This must have serous implications of the traditional view of parliament as a legislative body.'

*The report of the Ripon Commission into the
legislative process, 1993*

Since 1993 more directives, regulations and the Maastricht and Amsterdam Treaties have taken a heavy toll on British

By Stealth

'The truth is that new directives from Brussels are being passed into UK law with wholly inadequate scrutiny.

'Today MPs from both EU standing committees and the European Scrutiny Select Committee gave vivid examples of the impossibility of properly scrutinising the growing torrent of EU directives when faced with limited time and huge piles of poorly photocopied and baffling paperwork.

'Owen Paterson MP described how the European Select Committee is under pressure to process around one thousand documents a year. Because the committee only meets for half an hour per week each document gets an average of about one minute's scrutiny.

'As a result the Government is using its large majority on the Scrutiny Committee to ensure there is minimal discussion and force regulation through by stealth.

'Examples were cited of huge piles of paper arriving at the last minute before Committee meetings at which new laws are waved through on the nod . . . The European Working Time Directive that costs British business £2 billion ($3 billion) a year was put to parliament the day before the summer recess enabling the Government to slip the measure through with the absolute minimum of scrutiny . . .

'In effect the British people are being hoodwinked into accepting more and more red tape, whilst their elected representatives are powerless even to ensure it is properly discussed.'

Archie Norman MP, press release, 8.12.1999

independence, with the impact of the Treaty of Nice still to come.

Today it is likely that the 60 per cent figure reported by the Hansard Society has been far exceeded. A follow up study is to be published in 2001.

The hard-pressed House of Commons Scrutiny Committee reviewing this 'legislation', which is often carelessly drafted, cannot hope to assess it thoroughly or even at all. British Members of Parliament direct many questions to the British government, which may in turn redirect them to Brussels.

The House of Lords plays an outstanding role in reviewing Brussels legislation but again it is powerless to do more than warn and caution the government. One chairman of a Select Committee complained,

> 'We . . . wish to record our dissatisfaction with the attempts by the Council to secure political agreement on texts, which are frequently incomplete and deposited shortly before JHA [*Justice and Home Affairs*] meetings, thus seriously hampering effective scrutiny by national parliaments.'
>
> *Lord Tordoff's letter to Barbara Roche MP, House of*
> *Lords 12th Report on the European Communities,*
> *'Convention On Mutual Assistance In Criminal Matters*
> *Between The Member States Of The EU', 18.7.2000*

So far no Brussels law has ever been stopped in Westminster.

Who Are The Masters Now?

The importance of civil servants, both British and their counterparts from the other EU countries, has risen enormously. In London British civil servants *enact* Brussels regulations as

Qualified Majority Voting
Total votes: 87

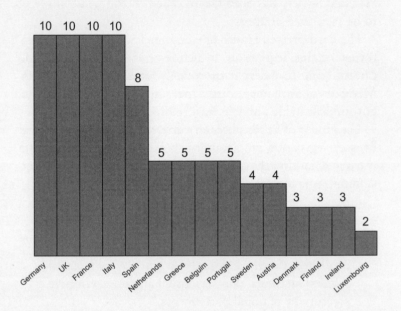

Germany To Have Blocking Vote

Once the EU has 27 members not only will votes in Council count, but also any measure will have to win 62 per cent of the total EU population. Germany, the most populous country, therefore will have an easy blocking vote for any measure. Under this rule Germany with 17 per cent needs the support of only two other large countries, say France and Italy, to block anything it does not like. Britain would need three other large countries to block a vote: a challenge indeed.

14

Statutory Instruments running at about 3,000 a year. These are not even subject to nominal democratic scrutiny.

In Brussels, British civil servants are active in over 250 committees that bargain their way, not to a British position, but to a *common* EU position (see page 251).

Their political 'masters' may vote on the civil servants' agreed positions in the European Council of Member States. There Britain can easily be outvoted on matters requiring qualified majority voting. For example, the national veto does not apply to any Single Market legislation. Britain has 10 votes out of 87. It takes 26 votes and a coalition of countries to block an issue.

Even where Britain has a national veto, for example on defence or policing, there is usually a price to pay in a totally different area for voting down a proposal backed by the Commission. The pressure is always strong to appear 'communitaire'.

The British voice can only be heard in Brussels in one way: horse-trading or bartering one item of sovereignty for another. The result is a constant haemorrhaging of independence.

Democracy in Britain has been seriously eroded by the loss of legislative independence. The British government is knowingly colluding in that loss.

Chapter 3

A COURT FOR EUROPE AND FOR BRITAIN

Crest of the European Court of Justice

A US Supreme Court Justice, Anthony Kennedy, warned the European Courts in 1999 that they were gaining too much power,

'European nations are surrendering their sovereignty on a scale never seen before . . . They've committed a tremendous amount of confidence, a tremendous amount of power . . . I think, too much, to the judiciary. All of the weight of developing this [democratic] consensus is being put on the courts, and this is dangerous for courts. You cannot overload a judicial structure with basic economic and social decisions.

'Remember, you are in a democratic society, and if you take on yourself all the important decisions in your society, ultimately you will cause a loss of respect for your Court, a loss of respect for judicial independence and a loss of respect for the law.'

From the Associated Press, 6.10.1999

A Court with a mission is a menace. A Supreme
Court with a mission is a tyranny.
Lord Neill of Bladon QC, 'The European Court of Justice,
A Case Study in Judicial Activism'

A Revolution Without Arms

From the beginning the EU was conceived as one state. And
from the beginning it had its own law court. The European
Court of Justice (ECJ) began work in 1952 for the European
Coal and Steel Community, the forerunner to the EEC.

The European Court of Justice has been working quietly in
the background for fifty years to extend the political power
of the EU and its predecessors. The Court's judgements are
the most important parts of the *acquis communautaire* (that
is all the principles, policies, laws practices, obligations and
objectives agreed or developed within the EU).

Over nearly five decades the Court has produced a substantial body of law. That law has begun to tower over the
legal systems of Member States.

The judgements of the Court have one intent which is to
further the purpose of the Treaty of Rome and take over all
the independent countries of Europe, 'to create an ever closer union' as the preamble states. It is a Court that has a far
ranging political impact as well as a judicial one.

The European Court of Justice

'Community law [is] a new body of law . . . independent, uniform in all the Member States of the Community, separate from, yet superior to national law.

'The Europe of the Communities . . . having become a frontier-free area in 1993 . . . is now moving towards political union following the adoption of the Maastricht Treaty . . . [with] ever greater influence for the case law which has built up over the four decades.

'The great innovation of the European Communities in comparison with previous attempts at European unification lies in the fact that the Community uses only the rule of law to achieve that end.'

http://europa.eu.int/cj/en/index.htm

One former European Court judge, G. Frederico Mancini, highlighted in The Making of a Constitution for Europe,

- The 'magnitude of the contribution made by the Court to the integration of Europe'
- The 'unprecedented law making powers' of the EU
- The way the EU Commission is leading 'the Court on the path towards further integration and increasing the Commission's power'
- The way the Court 'has sought to *constitutionalise* the Treaty [of Rome], to fashion a constitutional framework for a quasi-federal structure in Europe'

Ominously Mancini added that being in Luxembourg has helped, 'out of sight, out of mind.'

The Court creates legislation by making 'strained interpretations of the [treaty] texts,' as Lord Neill QC described in his case study.

From that Court there is no appeal and equally from that legislature there is no appeal. Its power is absolute. The men (for there are no women judges) who hold that immense power are both unelected and unaccountable. Effectively, democracy has been abolished.

The judges need have no judicial experience whatsoever and most have not. The paper qualifications to be an EU judge are the minimum required for its judiciary by each member country, in Britain that is ten years at the Bar. In practice, Britain requires more than simply time serving of its judges, and all British judges are highly practised in adversarial litigation.

In contrast, most EU judges have been academics or civil servants. Many have held other EU posts en route to becoming EU judges. They are not practised in adversarial litigation and they may never have defended a case.

World Pretensions

The EU judges see themselves as part of an elite of world judges, on a par with the US Supreme Court. They have exchanged formal visits with the US Supreme Court. In 1998 four US Justices visited the ECJ and in 2000 six judges of the ECJ spent a week in Washington, New York and Texas.

Judges from all EU countries make official visits to the ECJ – with the notable exception of British judges who, so far, have not made an official visit to the EU Court.

The EU judges do not visit the lower, national, courts of the EU.

The Case Load

The ECJ has already heard more than 8,600 cases.

In 1978 there were 200 new cases a year and by 1985 that had doubled. In 1999 543 new cases were filed.

To cope with the vast workload a preliminary court was created in 1989 called the Court of First Instance. On average a case takes 18 months to 2 years just for a preliminary ruling, and sometimes much longer.

Most cases are concerned with agriculture, approximation of laws, competition rules, the environment, freedom to provide services, social measures, and tax.

The Court hears cases against countries that fail to fulfil their EU obligations.

France, Italy, and Belgium are among the worst offenders with the Dutch, British, and Danes among the best. Since 1953 there have been over 1600 such cases.

Germany uses the Court most with over 1100 cases so far, nearly twice that of France. Between 1973 and 1999 Britain referred 291 cases.

How The Court Has Encroached On National Law Making

> 'European law was now a separate legal order tak-
> ing precedence over the laws in individual member
> states . . . In 1972 a group of us . . . had no difficulty
> in saying that UK law was henceforth to be subor-
> dinated to European law . . . The position was
> appreciated by our Courts. Soon after 1960 a
> number of decisions were made . . . which accepted
> the supremacy of European law even over our
> statutes . . . all this was well established when we
> entered the Community in 1973.'
>
> *Lord Wilberforce in a debate on the Maastricht Bill,*
> *House of Lords, June 1993*

The heart of the Treaty of Rome is Article 249. It recognises
the primacy of Community law,

> 'A regulation shall have general application. It shall
> be binding in its entirety and directly applicable in
> all Member States.
>
> 'A directive shall be binding, as to the result to be
> achieved, upon each Member State to which it is
> addressed, but shall leave to the national authorities
> the choice of form and methods.
>
> 'A decision shall be binding in its entirety upon
> those to whom it is addressed.'

Since 1957 the European Court has developed yet more
significant doctrines.

○ For the last 40 years all EU directives and ECJ judgements have had to be transferred into the law of member
  states within time limits. That is creating an EU legal

23

The Judges of Britain's Supreme Court

A Spanish academic, Professor Rodríguez Iglesias, has been the President of the Court, in Kirchberg, Luxembourg, since 1994 and he has spent over 15 years at the ECJ.

15 judges sit in the Court appointed by the governments of the Member States, one for each country. They sit for a renewable term of six years, likely to be increased under the Treaty of Nice to nine years. The judges choose one of their number to be President of the Court for a renewable term of three years.

The Court sits either in plenary (full) session or in six chambers of three judges. A Member State or an EU institution can ask for a plenary session.

The Court of First Instance has 15 judges in office for a renewable term of six years. The president is Bo Vesterdorf, formerly a Danish civil servant. Advocates General assist the ECJ: they deliver opinions on the cases.

The Commission is the prosecutor in the Court, described by the Court as the guardian of the Community's interests.

Because it has to use all 11 official languages of the Community the Court has an administration, including a translation and interpreting service.

code. The directives and judgements have to take effect *even if* they conflict with existing national law and *before* that national law can be amended. The doctrine of direct effect dates back to 1962 and the case of Van Gend en Loos.

Case 26/62

○ A 1991 judgement undermined national governments. Individuals now had the right to claim against their own national governments in the unelected, unaccountable European Court for failing to implement directives, *even when* those directives were not deemed to have direct effect.

Francovich and others v. Italy, Cases C6/90 and C9/90

The British government will have to pay over £100 million ($150 billion) to compensate Spanish fishermen. The Court ruled in 1991 that Britain had prevented the Spanish from fishing Britain's fish quotas by the 'illegal' British 1988 Merchant Shipping Act, passed by elected Members of Parliament. The Court ruled that the British Act was contrary to EU law.

The British government appealed to the British Court of Appeal in 1998, lost and appealed again to the British Law Lords in 1999 and lost again. Both British courts had to apply the EU court's ruling.

One of the Law Lords, Lord Hoffmann, said that the way Britain had discriminated against other Community nationals on the grounds of their nationality was 'prima facie flouting one of the most basic principles of Community law . . . Now justice requires that the wrong should be made good.'

○ Even if no EU measures have been taken, the European Court of Justice can declare areas of government to be outside the control of national governments (the doctrine of pre-emption). For example, because the Common Fisheries Policy existed, the European Court judged in 1981 that fish conservation was no longer a matter for nations, but only for the EU.

○ The Court can overrule the constitution of any EU nation state to achieve the end aim of one country. The German constitution says in Article 12a that '[Women] may on no account be assigned to military service involving armed combat.'

A court in Hanover confirmed that article of the German constitution. The European Court of Justice overruled the German court. Now women must be allowed to bear arms in the German army. A German newspaper reported,

> 'The 15 European judges are penetrating deeply into the structures of German defence and security policy.'
>
> *Handelsblatt, 12.1.2000*

Perhaps the most serious aspect of the betrayal meted on the British people in 1973 was handing supremacy over British law to a foreign court. Few have noticed its actions, few realise its implications but steadily the Court is strangling and overwhelming British democracy and British independence.

Future Courts

EU Branch Courts
In May 1998 the European Court of Justice issued a press release on proposals for 'the future of the judicial system of the EU.' The Court was becoming overburdened with cases.

That was about to be made worse by the launch of the euro, the Amsterdam Treaty and perhaps by even more countries joining the EU.

The Court therefore wants to have its branches in every country to issue preliminary rulings on cases referred from 'local', that is national, Courts.

The European Court Of Human Rights

On the face of it this Court has nothing to do with the EU. It is a child of the Council of Europe. Yet increasingly the EU Commission is influencing the work of the Council of Europe. Already one MEP has written a paper proposing that the European Court of Human Rights be turned into the Appeal Court for the European Court of Justice. It is still too early for that given that the first Court covers 41 countries while the later covers just 15. But it is probable that if and when the EU expands, as it intends, then there will be a close relationship between the two Courts.

Speaking on the 50th anniversary of the foundation of the Council of Europe, Europe's primary 'human rights' body, the president of its parliamentary assembly Lord Johnston said,

> 'The defence of democracy is a never-ending task . . .
> The dominant characteristic of the Council's action
> in the next five years should be interference in the
> internal affairs of member states.'

The Council has lived up to Lord Johnston's expectations.

The Labour government adopted the European Convention on Human Rights into English and Welsh law effective from 2nd October 2000. It is a fundamental change to the British constitution and will have wide-ranging implications for the British judicial system, transferring unprecedented power from Parliament to the judges.

If an Act passed by the democratically elected British parliament is deemed by the European Court to be 'incompatible with the European convention' it can force the British government to amend it. Thus judges sitting in Strasbourg overrule the elected representatives of the British people.

As the Lord Chancellor, Lord Irvine, wrote in 1998 in *Public Law*,

> 'The strong interpretative techniques that will be applied by British Courts to British statutes in Human Rights cases will strain the meaning of words or read in words which are not there.'

The European Convention on Human Rights 1950 was drawn up by the Council of Europe to take the first steps for the collective enforcement of rights in the United Nations Universal Declaration of Human Rights of 1948. Britain was the first country to ratify it.

The Convention arrived early in Scotland, in May 1999. According to Alistair Bonnington of the School of Law at Glasgow University,

> 'It is clear that the Scottish Supreme Courts are now, in effect, constitutional Courts. They can set aside legislation of the Scottish parliament and declare actions of the Scottish Ministers to be illegal . . . taken at its extreme Scots judges, by accident or design, now have a degree of influence that politicians will almost certainly live to regret.'
>
> *The Times, 15.2.2000*

Judges Of The European Court Of Human Rights

The judges come from the 41 countries of the Council of Europe. 17 of them trained in what were then Communist countries including the USSR and who had to be Communists to rise in the system. Their systems of 'law' could not be further from that practised in Britain. The Parliamentary Assembly of the Council of Europe elects the judges for a term of six years. They are said to be independent of their own countries and impartial.

Four guest member countries may in due course be able to contribute a judge each. They are: Armenia, Azerbaijan, Belarus, and Bosnia-Herzegovina.

Chapter 4

BYE BYE OLD BAILEY

The Old Bailey is the most important crown court in England. The court can try crimes from any part of the country. Established as a Session House in 1539 and rebuilt in 1774, the Old Bailey became known as the Central Criminal Court. The building was demolished in 1902 and today the Old Bailey stands on the site of Newgate Prison.

Improved internal security calls for much greater integration and consistency. This is both a logical and necessary step. We have an internal market, we are introducing a single currency, and next, all EU citizens have to be guaranteed the right to move freely and to live without fears of threats to their safety.

Tarja Halonen, the Finnish Foreign Minister, at the
Tampere Summit, October 1999

How The EU Is Introducing A Criminal Justice System, Which Could Lead To A Police State

The Tampere Summit in Finland in October 1999 was the first EU Council completely dedicated to justice and home affairs. It marked the acceleration of the process to create a European legal system and a European police force and superimpose them on the national legal systems and police forces.

Britain and Ireland have the most to lose. They are the only two EU countries with legal systems based on common law with tough safeguards against extreme state power. They have habeas corpus, trial by jury and police independent of the judiciary.

The EU Commission is trying to impose one continental style system of criminal law throughout the EU, though it

EU Excuse Number 1:
'Criminals Are Cashing In On The Four Freedoms'

The EU Commission says organised crime is gaining ground in the EU. Mafia-type groups are taking advantage of the free movement of capital, goods, people and services within the EU. They exploit anomalies, legal loopholes, and differences in legislation between the EU Member States. Groups of mainly EU 'citizens' are operating across the Continent.

Border controls are virtually gone and there is no EU police. The existence of co-operating national police forces is conveniently ignored.

The Commission wants an EU strategy to prevent and control organised crime.

denies any such thing. A continental system would overwhelm and replace the British criminal justice system with a codified law and a continental model of inquisitorial courts in which the state is all-powerful and the police are an arm of the judiciary.

British judges would impose the rule of Brussels and the *British* police would report to Brussels.

To avoid arousing public disquiet, especially in Britain, the EU has moved cautiously. If the EU succeeds, the repercussions will be Orwellian. All civil and criminal law, the courts, and the police will be under the authority either of the EU Commission in Brussels or the European Court of Justice in Strasbourg. It will be the makings of a police state.

Step one was to start to remove national border controls. The EU says borders are barriers to the four freedoms of the Treaty of Rome. A Single Market cannot work if there are barriers in the way. Nearly all border controls have now gone, except in Britain and Ireland.

Step two is the logical conclusion that if there are no 'internal' borders then there has to be one legal system with one police force, or as it is described in the Amsterdam treaty, 'an area of freedom, justice and security' (Article 2).

In practice, the two steps are not distinct but overlap and all the time the EU is chipping away at national judicial freedoms across a wide front.

Since the Labour Party came into power in Britain in 1997 the EU has had an ally and the British legal system is being eroded from within.

An EU Criminal Code In Embryo

'In the eyes of euro-paranoiacs, the Corpus Juris has become evidence of a sinister plot to undermine and destroy our legal system. I have to say that belief in

EU Excuse Number 2: Fraud

The Commission is using the excuse of endemic fraud in the Brussels' system to introduce an EU criminal justice system. Fraud starts at the top. In March 1999 a report from a committee of independent experts appointed by the European Parliament, which investigated corruption and cronyism in the Commission immediately led to the resignation of all the EU Commissioners.

Despite the resignations, the Commission still had serious flaws according to the follow-up report published in September 1999, including lax control of EU funds, unaccountability, heavy reliance on bought-in advisers, and biased, if not corrupt, recruitment policies.

The experts declared, 'The EU's administration has a tendency to put the development of ideas above the exercising of control . . . [the Commission] sees itself as more visionary than managerial.'

The experts proposed 90 changes, including an EU prosecutor with *unlimited powers* to investigate offences committed by EU officials. The prosecutor would be backed by a team of prosecutors in Member States to look into abuses of EU funds. The network would become 'an indivisible and independent European Prosecutions Office.'

The report says plans for a 'single legal area' should be completed by 2004 or 2005 in time for the next enlargement of the EU.

Allegations regarding Fraud, Mismanagement and Nepotism
in the European Commission, 15.3.1999
Reform of the Commission Analysis of current practice and pro-
posals for tackling mismanagement, irregularities and fraud,
10.9.1999

such a plot is no more justified than belief in the
authenticity of the protocols of the elders of Zion.'
Lord Goodhart QC in the House of Lords,
Hansard, 25.11.1999

Corpus Juris was the subject of an EU report published in
April 1997 and written by eight academic lawyers, experts in
criminal law, one of whom was British, Professor John
Spencer of Cambridge University. It is part of the *European
Legal Area Project* launched by the European Commission
(Directorate General XX) in 1990. Like most EU reports,
only a few specialists would normally read it. But by chance
a wider audience came to know of it.

One man drew attention to Corpus Juris. Torquil Dick-
Erikson, a British journalist living in Italy who writes on legal
affairs, attended the Commission's invitation-only seminar in
Spain in April 1997 to launch Corpus Juris.

Dick-Erikson reported that at the Spanish seminar there
was no mention or discussion of the impact that Corpus Juris
would make on the British system of law. It was as though
Britain's legal system did not exist. He raised the issue and his
points were ignored.

Corpus Juris was billed as 'the embryo of a future
European criminal code' and Jose Maria Gil-Robles,
President of the European Parliament, repeated that message
to the seminar adding that the code would eventually cover
all types of criminal activity, which he listed.

The EU Commission and its apologists have since passed
Corpus Juris off as simply a research study into ways to combat fraud against the EU and of limited scope.

But it was not: two years later the European Parliament
resolved,

> 'The Parliament . . . calls for the gradual establish-
> ment of a European criminal law system in which

account is taken of Member States' legal traditions. It contemplates the creation of an independent European Public Prosecutor, initially to centralise judicial information on transitional investigations under way relating to offences covered by the European criminal law system in order to ensure better co-ordination of national investigations. At a later stage the European Public Prosecutor might be given responsibility to open investigations and bring proceedings involving offences covered by the European criminal law system.'

A4-0091/99, adopted on 13.4.1999

Dropped at the last minute from the Treaty of Nice, was the appointment of a European Public Prosecutor appointed for a non-renewable term of six years with no national veto,

'The European Public Prosecutor shall be responsible for detecting, prosecuting and bringing to judgement the perpetrators of offences prejudicial to the Community's financial interests and their accomplices and for exercising the functions of prosecutor in the national courts of the Member States.'

No doubt that will resurface in 2004. An EU criminal justice system is on the way.

What Is Corpus Juris?

'The great principles of Habeas Corpus and trial by jury are the supreme protection invented by the British people for ordinary individuals against the state. The power of the executive to cast a man into prison without formulating any charge known to the law, and particularly to deny him judgement by his peers for an indefinite period, is in the highest degree odious, and is the foundation of all totalitarian governments. Nothing can be more abhorrent to democracy. This is really the test of civilisation.'

Winston Churchill to the Home Secretary about the Mosley family, 21.11.1943

Corpus Juris would introduce a criminal code for the investigation, prosecution and punishment of fraud and other crimes against the EU's finances. The code would apply to all the EU Member States. Once introduced for fraud it could rapidly be extended to every other type of crime.

The 35 articles of *Corpus Juris, A Draft Criminal Code And Code Of Procedure* define crimes of fraud with penalties of up to seven years in jail; establish new EU institutions; and procedures for investigations, committals, prosecutions, detentions before trial of up to nine months, trials, and execution of sentences.

Under Corpus Juris a suspect could be arrested anywhere in the EU, held in jail without a public hearing and without any evidence produced against him, for indefinite periods of time, and transported around the EU at will. When eventually the accused is tried a professional judge, without a jury, would declare him innocent or guilty.

Corpus Juris

Extradition proceedings within the EU are abolished because 'the territory of the Member States of the Union constitutes a single legal area', Article 18.1.

An all-powerful European Public Prosecutor (EPP) has jurisdiction throughout the EU assisted by *existing* national public prosecutors, Article 18.5. He will be 'independent as regards both national authorities and community institutions', Article 18.2. He will be 'responsible for investigation, prosecution, committal to trial, presenting the prosecution case at trial, and the execution of sentences.'

In custody without charge. The European Public Prosecutor, his deputies in Brussels or locally have the power to remand someone in custody or on bail for up to six months, renewable for another three months, where there are reasonable grounds to suspect the accused has committed an offence (in Articles 1 to 8) or good reasons to believe he might commit such an offence or from fleeing after committing it, Article 20.3g.

The Law Society declared,

> 'This will introduce to the English law for the first time the concept of a person being held in custody without charge, making massive in-roads into safeguards in place under UK legislation for those in custody.'
>
> *In evidence to the House of Lords Select Committee on European Communities 9th Report 'Prosecuting Fraud On The Communities' Finances—The Corpus Juris', 18.5.1999*

EU arrest warrants. The EPP can instruct a 'national judge' to issue a European warrant for arrest 'valid across the whole territory', Article 24.1b.

State Defence. A new type of judge in the Member States would ensure that defendants' rights are protected. The judge of freedoms would exercise judicial control over the investigatory activities of the EPP and ensure, for example, that the obligations of the European Convention on Human Rights were met (Article 25). But such a judge could easily become a creature of the European Public Prosecutor. He could feed the EPP with the necessary information to justify coercive action and it would be granted.

Habeas Corpus. Significantly and ominously, the judges do not scrutinise the *prima facie* evidence against a suspect. Habeas Corpus, enacted in 1679 because of public outcry at a number of abusive arrests, would be quashed for criminal defendants. Habeas Corpus literally means presenting the accused physically in court so that all may see him, usually within 48 hours of arrest, so that the evidence against him is reviewed in public.

No juries, no magistrates. The courts 'must consist of professional judges . . . not simple jurors or lay magistrates', Article 26.1. Trial by Jury, a British freedom since 1215, and the independent magistrate system are to be abolished.

The End Of The Sovereign State

The Faculty of Advocates (Scottish barristers) considered *Corpus Juris* would have profound political implications. They said in evidence to the House of Lords Select Committee on Corpus Juris,

> 'The width of the proposals is such that they do not merely have a direct bearing on the sovereignty of the United Kingdom. They, in fact, result in *surrendering the sovereignty of the State* in relation to a range of criminal offences.'

The London Criminal Courts Solicitors' Association (LCCSA) agreed that,

> 'In constituting itself part of a single legal area the United Kingdom would be transferring powers, such as the issue of arrest warrants, to an external authority. Those powers were attributes of statehood. They should not be transferred without the political decision having been taken, through con-

stitutional means, that *the United Kingdom no longer wished to regard itself as a sovereign state.*'

The British government believed that,

'Many of its proposals would be *difficult to square with important principles of UK law*. The creation of a separate prosecution authority with no accountability to Parliament would raise difficult issues. The insertion of inquisitorial procedures into a largely adversarial system raised fundamental issues for procedure in criminal trials and the admissibility of evidence.'

The Lords Condemned The European Public Prosecutor

'The Corpus Juris would invest enormous power in the hands of the EPP. He . . . would be able to exercise substantial coercive powers in relation to the citizen and in doing so would be independent of national governments and the Community institutions. Certain of the EPP's activities would be supervised by the judge of freedoms. Yet, except in disciplinary proceedings before the European Court of Justice and possibly by way of judicial review before national courts, he would not be accountable to anyone. There seems to be general agreement that this is politically unacceptable. The EPP should be answerable to a democratically elected body, national parliaments and/or the European Parliament. The latter has acknowledged the sensitivity of the notion of a European Public Prosecutor and has proposed that the EPP might be introduced gradually, initially to co-ordinate anti-fraud procedures and to superintend Europol. We would need to be persuaded that such a role was necessary and could not be carried out by an existing body or bodies.'

The Lords Condemned Corpus Juris

' . . . the more fundamental and strongest objections related to Part II (Criminal Procedure). The approaches taken in the United Kingdom to the investigation and prosecution of crime are quite different in several respects from those in other Member States and the model proposed in the *Corpus Juris*. Under the latter, for example, the functions of investigation and prosecution of offences and execution of sentences would be combined in the hands of a European Public Prosecutor (EPP). The trial would be in a national court but before a specialist judge, with no jury. The Commission could be involved as a *partie civile* in the proceedings . . .

'The procedure in the *Corpus Juris* seeks to marry the inquisitorial and adversarial/written and oral traditions of the Member States, though the result is probably closer to the Continental European than the Anglo-Saxon model . . .

'Last but not least, the rights of the defendant seem largely to be set indirectly by reference to (minimum) international standards. This is in marked contrast to the detail given to the powers of the prosecution. We see a real danger that the *Corpus Juris* will be too much prosecution driven, with insufficient account being taken of the rights of the defence. The accused has a place in an 'area of freedom, security and justice' . . .

' . . . the powers of remand given to the agents of the EPP (who can) request a person's remand in custody without charge or remand on bail for a period of up to six months, renewable for three months . . . the prospect that an individual may be held in custody, without charge, for up to nine months is totally unacceptable.'

Extracts from House of Lords Select Committee on European Communities 9th Report 'Prosecuting Fraud On The Communities' Finances – The Corpus Juris', 18.5.1999.

Blair's Government Assists Steps To A Police State

'Only the most compelling grounds of public interest could ever justify the abandonment of trial by jury in any area. The purpose is to cut costs. It has nothing to do with justice. It is a bad proposal.'

Lord Steyn, one of Britain's most senior judges

Independently of the EU, the Blair government has attacked both the jury system and lay magistrates with the apparent aim of abolishing or severely restricting them. These changes would 'harmonise' the British justice system with the continental court system. Is the Labour government trying to make Britain's legal system fit the continental mould or is it saving money at the expense of justice?

Jack Straw, the Labour Home Secretary, has tried to limit the rights of defendants in England and Wales to choose trial by jury and be judged innocent or guilty by their peers, not by professional judges paid by the state.

Straw's plans met widespread and deep-seated opposition and were rejected by the House of Lords. They would affect around 18,000 defendants every year charged with offences that can be tried either by magistrates or the Crown Courts. The list of middle-ranking crimes includes burglary, shoplifting and common assault and at present it is open to the accused to elect for a jury hearing. Under Straw's proposals magistrates would decide if the crime merited trial by jury.

Lay magistrates have been the cornerstone of the British justice system for more than 600 years. They could be phased out under Jack Straw's plans. All but about 90 of the country's 30,000 magistrates, whose office dates back to the Justices of the Peace Act of 1361, are lay people. They hear over 90 per cent of criminal cases. Paid professionals would replace them.

The Labour government believes that paid professionals would be cheaper than the current system because stipendiaries are quicker to reach a verdict and sit alone rather than in threes. To prove the case Jack Straw and Lord Irvine, the Lord Chancellor, commissioned a review by an academic at Bristol University, to be published at the beginning of 2001. It is a 'time and motion' study of lay magistrates compared with paid professionals.

The government is likely to meet fierce resistance to a plan, which sacrifices justice on the altar of saving money.

Small Steps To The EU's Criminal Justice System

> 'People have a right to expect the Union to address the threat to their freedom and legal rights posed by serious crime . . . The joint mobilisation of police and judicial resources is needed to guarantee that there is no hiding place for criminals or the proceeds of crime within the Union.'
>
> *European Council's 'Tampere Milestones', October 1999*

When public outcry in Britain blocked the introduction of Corpus Juris, the EU side-stepped and pressed ahead with other ways to create the 'area of freedom, security and justice' of the Amsterdam Treaty. Some of these proposals make good sense but taken as a whole they could overwhelm the British legal system. The Labour government has readily agreed to most of them.

EU countries can intercept British telephones and e-mails

> '[The Convention] . . . will enhance the ability of UK courts to deal with international criminals. It simplifies procedures where evidence from abroad is needed in the UK, and enables UK authorities to assist in provision of evidence abroad. It also allows greater use of video links in criminal trials so that witnesses may in some circumstances no longer have to travel abroad to give evidence.'
>
> *Jack Straw in a Home Office press release, 29.5.2000*

Each EU country will recognise the judicial decisions of other EU countries with a minimum of formality under *the Convention on Mutual Assistance in Criminal Matters between Member States*. That will include judicial decisions taken *before* as well as *after* conviction. Britain agreed to the Convention on 29th May 2000.

The House of Commons European Scrutiny Committee concluded of an early draft,

> 'It is questionable how far mutual recognition is appropriate where no agreement on common legal concepts or substantive criminal law exists.'
>
> *1999*

EU governments will have the power to trawl through the

personal records of British citizens suspected of criminal conduct. EU governments will be able to request the intercept of e-mail, fax, and telephone of suspected criminals in other EU countries.

'A significant, and sensitive, development,' a House of Lords Select Committee called it.

12th Report, 'Convention On Mutual Assistance In Criminal Matters Between The Member States Of The European Union,' 18.7.2000

Where other countries can intercept communications *without* needing British technical help Britain will usually have 96 hours to answer the request. Consent will be implied unless or until Britain explicitly demands the interception be stopped. The interception would be lawful throughout those 96 hours, or maximum eight days, *even if* no express consent has been given.

Therefore some short-term interceptions could take place *without any British authority whatsoever*, even though Britain should be made aware of the interception. The Convention relied, and perhaps unwisely, on good faith to preserve sovereignty in this critical area.

Britain can refuse to agree to requests if they clash with British law (which in any case is being eroded). The Convention requires that usually states 'shall undertake to comply with requests' for help. In practice it may be difficult, though not impossible, for Britain to refuse a request.

The Labour government championed this Convention in part because it avoids introducing one law across the EU. But despite the government's hopes, the EU Justice and Home Affairs Council recorded on 29th May 2000 that there may be 'conflicting national penal codes (which) may require some *harmonisation* of legal standards.'

The Commission says the Convention will help the investigation of organised crime, paedophilia and terrorism. In fact its terms can apply to *any* offence. The House of Commons European Scrutiny Committee condemned it because the Convention does not say what sort of crimes could possibly justify such intrusive surveillance.

Even the European Parliament raised the issue that cross-border surveillance requests could be misused to pursue minor offenders or even to keep watch on political opponents.

The Convention was not seriously changed and there is little to stop any EU police force saying, 'Here's a telephone line we want to tap.'

The EU Fingerprint Databank

> ' . . . compulsory fingerprinting is a significant interference with the individual right to respect for private life and requires a lawful justification.'
>
> *A conclusion from House of Lords report, 'Fingerprinting illegal immigrants: extending the Eurodac convention',*
>
> *8.6.1999*

Britain is likely to sign up to the EU computer database of fingerprints of all asylum applicants over the age of 14. It will be operated by the Commission on behalf of the Member States. Called *Eurodac* it will be operational in 2001.

Eurodac, a computerised fingerprint recognition system, will make it easy to identify which Member State has allowed in an asylum applicant first and is responsible for processing their immigration claim.

The British government expects fingerprinting will stop other EU member countries turning a blind eye to bogus asylum seekers as long as they travel on to another country and become somebody else's problem. It may also deter the substantial problem of people 'asylum shopping' round the EU looking for the best welfare deal.

The danger is that once the EU Commission has that database of fingerprints it will be easy to extend the system to uses other than asylum seekers. *Eurodac* establishes a principle which may prove to be an unwelcome one.

The European Judicial Network

The European Judicial Network (EJN) began work in September 1998 and is yet another way to amalgamate the national criminal systems. The aim is the laudable one of improving co-operation between the judicial authorities on criminal matters. The Network meets regularly and acts as a one-stop-shop to provide legal and practical information to practitioners in their own countries and abroad. Each country has its own contact points. Again it may prove to be a stage on the road to one EU criminal justice system.

Half way to a European Public Prosecutor: Eurojust

To get around British resistance to an EU Public Prosecutor, France and Germany promoted Eurojust in September 1999. Britain agreed to it.

Eurojust may become the prosecuting authority, for the whole EU. According to the Commission and the treaty of Nice,

> [Eurojust will co-ordinate] 'national prosecuting authorities and of police officers [and] may one day . . . support criminal investigations in organised crime cases.'

National prosecutors, magistrates and police officers from each country will make up Eurojust with its own secretariat. It will be the judicial arm of the European Police Force (Europol), the EU's anti fraud office (Olaf) and the European

Eurojust: Backdoor To Corpus Juris
HANSARD
Written Answers

5 Nov 1999: Column: 370

Mr. Charles Clarke (Norwich South): As my right hon. Friend the Prime Minister reported to the House in his statement on 19th October 1999, *Official Report*, columns 253-65, "Corpus Juris" was not a topic for discussion at the Tampere European Council, nor did the European Council endorse any of the specific proposals in "Corpus Juris" such as creating a European penal code or a European public prosecutor. There was a brief discussion on whether to examine one Corpus Juris proposal, the idea of creating a European Public Prosecutor, concerned only with protecting the financial interests of the Community, but this was not pursued. The conclusions of the European Council were aimed at achieving

"better compatibility and more convergence between the legal systems of member states".

In particular, the European Council concluded that the principle of mutual recognition, put forward by the United Kingdom, should become

"the cornerstone of judicial co-operation in both civil and criminal matters within the Union".

The European Council also agreed to create an intergovernmental unit, 'Eurojust', to work in liaison with Europol and the European Judicial Network to help to facilitate

"the proper co-ordination of national prosecuting authorities, and support national criminal investigations in cases of serious organised crime".

Judicial Network (EJN). The unit should start work at the end of 2001.

Eurojust's powers have yet to be agreed including its organisation, composition, degree of independence, headquarters and funding.

EU countries agreed that Eurojust should not *at this stage* include any initiative on preliminary investigation into crimes. *At first* it will be limited to co-ordinating enquiries to speed up procedures.

Only Britain wishes to restrict Eurojust to major transnational crimes. Will it succeed? Or will sovereignty be eroded further?

Corpus Juris In 117 Doses

In the first months of 2000, Antonio Vitorino, the EU Justice Commissioner, toured the capitals of the EU and sold the idea of a scoreboard, or progress plan, to speed up the EU's area of freedom, security and justice. Items on the scoreboard include much of Corpus Juris, and more besides, but in 117 small doses. Here are some of them:

○ **An EU criminal record system**
The EU says it is an absolute and immediate priority to *harmonise* the data collected by national security services across the EU on crimes and suspected criminals. Europol is working on it. Once criminal records are in the same format it will of course be much easier to apply uniform sanctions across the EU.

○ **Private tax information to be passed abroad**
The Commission wants to ban people with known links to organised crime from bidding for public subsidies or licences. Organised tax fraud, such as VAT and excise fraud, especially across frontiers is targeted.

HANSARD
The British Government Dissembles
The House of Commons Select Committee
on Home Affairs

26 Oct 1999:

Mr. Gerald Howarth (Aldershot): You said that the United Kingdom had also supported the creation of a European public prosecutor which some would say is a further indication of the way in which we are going. One of the keys of the *corpus juris* is that there should be a European public prosecutor to whom effectively national prosecutors should be under a duty to assist. You kind of pooh pooh it. In Article 46 of the Presidency's conclusions it says, "To reinforce the fight against serious organised crime, the European Council has agreed that a unit (EUROJUST) should be set up composed of national prosecutors, magistrates, or police officers of equivalent competence, detached from each Member State according to its legal system. EUROJUST should have the task of facilitating the proper consultation of national prosecuting authorities and of supporting criminal investigations in organised crime cases." The point I put to you, Home Secretary, is that those of a suspicious disposition might say herein lies the seed of a future European public prosecution service.

Mr. Winnick: Another conspiracy.

Mr. Howarth: How do you respond to that?(*Mr Straw*) The words mean what they say. We signed up to that because it is a network of national prosecutors.

This is another way of attacking national tax records: the EU wants national tax authorities to exchange information on individuals with each other and with national judiciaries. The deadline is the end of 2002.

○ **EU to tackle all crime**
Major crimes, particularly fraud against the EU, has been the limit of the EU's apparent interest but in this little measure the EU says that to prevent re-offending, 'careers' in crime need to be interrupted at the earliest opportunity. So the Commission has decided its remit goes beyond serious crime to all crime, large or small. It wants greater use of non-judicial measures and non-custodial sentences. The deadline is the end of 2001.

○ *Approximating* **criminal law**
National laws on organised crime, terrorism, and drug trafficking will be made almost the same or 'approximated'. Deadlines will be set for each type of crime. The first of these should be completed by the end of 2000. This is a long term project with crimes 'approximated' at a rate of roughly one per Presidency, that is one every four years.

○ **Combining investigative resources**
The EU is studying national control of electronic surveillance, undercover agents, promises of immunity and plea-bargaining. The excuse is the fight against illegal immigration networks. An action group from national authorities may be set up to combine existing resources. Execution is expected by the end of 2001.

○ **More European Police**
The Commission wants a bigger role for Europol and police from all the EU countries working together in

joint teams to support national operations, see also page 65. Implementation is expected by July 2001.

○ **Redefining guilt**
Money laundering needs more powers of investigation, the Commission thinks. If a suspect should have realised that the assets in question had been earned through criminal activity, then he will be declared guilty. Implementation is expected by the end of 2000.

○ **Tax havens attacked**
Member States will have to enforce EU measures against tax havens within their territory but *outside* the EU, and that includes the Channel Islands and the Isle of Man. The EU's targets are trust funds and other ways supposedly used to hide an owner's identity. A standard form of agreement should be in place by the end of 2001 to use in 'negotiations' with offshore and onshore financial centres and tax havens, see also page 178

○ **Revealing who uses the internet**
To combat money laundering on the Internet and the use of electronic money, the Commission wants electronic payment and paging systems to provide it with detailed information on senders and receivers by the end of 2001.

○ **Limiting the use of cash**
The Commission wants a limit on the use of cash by anyone in the EU. The excuse is that paying in cash could camouflage the conversion of the proceeds of crime into other assets. Adoption is expected by the end of 2003.

○ **The EU to protect informants**
The Commission wants a uniform approach to the protection of witnesses and of current and past members of

criminal organisations prepared to co-operate with the Courts to provide evidence leading to the confiscation of money and goods. This should be in force by 2001.

○ **Eurowarrants and fast extradition**
National governments are expected to adopt measures by 2002 to ensure that extradition requests are dealt with rapidly. A request from one country would lead to the immediate arrest and removal of an alleged offender *without any scrutiny by the British courts* under fast-track extradition through mutual recognition of arrest warrants and convictions, or a new eurowarrant system. The Commission wants a single EU area for extradition by 2010, so that there can be no interference or protection by national governments in moving a suspect from one part of the EU to another. Today British courts have to be convinced that the jurisdiction to which an offender is to be extradited offers a fair trial and that a crime has been committed. Tomorrow that will not apply.

○ **Minimum standards of evidence**
The Commission wants minimum standards (but how low?) for decisions on the admissibility of proof so that evidence collected in one country can be laid before the courts of another EU country. This should be in place by the end of 2004.

○ **EU law to reach candidate countries before they join**
The EU wants to extend its legal system as far as possible to all the candidate countries notably in Eastern Europe and at this stage by co-operation.

The End Of Freedom?

Once the national veto on justice and home affairs has been abolished – and it is being eroded as treaty succeeds treaty – there will be nothing to stop Brussels imposing the EU legal system with a European police force of officers from all the member countries to enforce it.

A British government, which agrees to this, will be handing over a democratic nation to a totalitarian regime.

It is at the least curious that at a time when the British legal system is under direct attack from the EU Commission the Labour government is also trying to remove key British safeguards. Nor has the government said it will defend Britain's national veto on justice and home affairs. It is difficult to avoid the conclusion that the British government and the EU are working to the same plan.

Chapter 5

INSPECTOR CLOUSEAU COMES TO SCOTLAND YARD

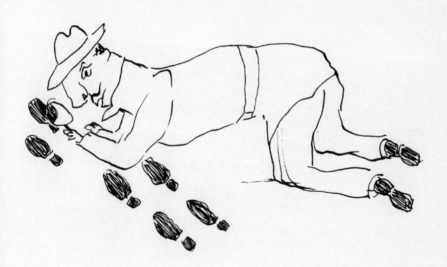

States place themselves in an impossible position,
for by insisting on the legal inviolability of borders
they only handicap their law enforcement agencies.
Jorgen Storbeck, Director of Europol to the British Police
Federation, 21.9.1999

A few years ago the idea of an EU police force would have
been laughable. Even more ridiculous would have been the
notion that the British police would take their orders from
Brussels and that French or German officers would police
Britain. Yet this prospect is well on the way to fruition.

Europol is a new organisation controlled by the EU
Member States. It analyses serious cross border crime, mainly drug related. If that were to be its future Europol would be
uncontentious. But Europol is beginning to challenge the
authority of national police forces and the right of the EU
nations to police their own territory, under the powers of the
Amsterdam Treaty.

Already in its short life Europol has some attributes which
give cause for alarm. Europol officers have diplomatic immunity. In other words, they are above the law. Diplomatic
immunity for Europol officers slipped quietly into British law
via a British Statutory Instrument in 1997 (No. 2973) bypassing the Houses of Parliament. It said,

> 'Such persons shall enjoy immunity from suit and
> legal process in respect of acts, including words

written or spoken, done by them in the exercise of their official functions, except in respect of civil liability in the case of damage arising from a road traffic accident caused by them.'

If Europol officers are involved in wrongful arrest, perhaps using undue force, or destruction to homes and property, there can be no redress. In time the very existence of diplomatic immunity may lead to arrogance and excesses on the part of Europol officers. Diplomatic immunity for police officers is a first in the history of policing Britain.

Foreign police officers have operated in Britain for many years but usually against their own nationals and only by agreement with the British police. Now the EU Commission would like foreign police officers, who are above the law, as well as police from other EU countries to be able to operate in mixed forces against the British on British soil.

Paradoxically and nonsensically having given Europol officers diplomatic immunity the government then told a House of Lords Select Committee that were operations to be carried out by Europol officers then,

'Their status in this country would be that of ordinary members of the public. They would have the same liability as other members of the public.'

Paras. 10 and 13 of Explanatory Memorandum on the Draft Convention on Mutual Assistance in Criminal Matters between the Member States of the EU submitted by the Home Office, 13.12.1999

It is doubtful if the European Court of Justice would agree with that.

One British Police Force?

Changes in British policing may already be moving in the direction of a national police force with political consequences. Today the British police rely for their authority on officers coming from the community, being part of the community and policing with the agreement of the community. There is no central police force, political influence is low and police officers are not above the law.

Pressure to save money, as well as the break up of Britain into EU regions, is now challenging the independence of the British police. It is driving the debate on combining police forces, perhaps to the point of creating a single national police force. Dangerously, these changes are happening at the same time as the EU's drive to create one European police force with overarching powers.

Chief Superintendent Peter Gammon, president of the Superintendents Association of England and Wales, told his annual conference in September 2000 that there should be just eight forces within ten years. Gammon was concerned about cost and he wanted to catch more criminals.

Former Superintendent David Hodges of the Thames Valley Police went further when interviewed in *The Times* on 14th July 1999 suggesting that Britain's 43 police forces would soon be amalgamated into one,

> 'I really fear that, I think it would become highly politicised, in a way that chief constables are spared at the moment, and . . . it would erode individual liberties. But we are increasingly becoming part of Europe, and all European police forces are national. We will sooner or later have to conform.'

Hodges expected that Britain with the only unarmed police

forces in the EU might equally be under pressure to carry firearms.

Another troubling development was the change in the make-up of Police Authorities under the 1996 Police Act. Local magistrates and independent people no longer dominate the Police Authorities. They gave way to locally elected councillors. That has a special significance when the EU is steadily making inroads into British local authorities, most of which now have direct and increasing links with Brussels.

Europol Nuts And Bolts

Europol has its headquarters in The Hague in a heavily fortified quadrangular building, once a Jesuit school. In the Second World War this building was a Nazi – and Gestapo – headquarters.

Today it has about 175 permanent staff, which will increase to 350 by 2002. 17 of the staff are British. There are 45 liaison officers including four British police officers from the National Criminal Intelligence Service (NCIS).

Europol has 'national' units in each member country. In Britain the unit is in the International Division of NCIS at its London headquarters. It has 12 staff, and all are NCIS employees.

Europol costs the Member States about £16 million ($24 million) in 2000 and £18 million ($27 million) in 2001.

The History Of Europol

1984 – When the police project began at the Fontainebleau Summit it was so contentious, even as a co-operative venture, that debate between governments took several years because some countries, notably Germany, wanted a police force with powers of investigation throughout the EU, others like Britain did not.

1994 – The European Drugs Agency began operations. It was purely co-operative 'to support Member States . . . in the fight against drugs and associated money laundering.'

1998 – The European Drugs Agency changed its name to Europol.

1999 – Europol acquired legal identity enabling it to operate beyond its original remit as a drugs unit.

Europol Today

A former German police officer, Jorgen Storbeck, has run Europol since it began as the drugs unit in 1994. Europol's deputy directors are from Belgium, Luxembourg, Italy, Britain and France.

Senior police officers from each of the Member States are now forming a multinational command for Europol.

A permanent EU task force of police chiefs is being set up. It will parallel a similar organisation of the chiefs of the defence staff, which already operates in Brussels.

Britain and Germany make the most use of Europol. The British police and Customs and Excise see it as a useful form of Interpol. Europol may sound the same as Interpol, and probably deliberately so, but it is very different. While Interpol is purely co-operative, Europol is rapidly moving towards having some executive authority.

Europol's present mandate is to fight organised criminals involved in:

○ Illicit drug trafficking (over half its present activity)
○ Crimes involving secret immigration networks

○ Vehicle trafficking
○ Trafficking in human beings including child pornography
○ Forging money
○ Trafficking in radioactive and nuclear substances
○ Terrorism
○ Money-laundering

Beyond Co-operation

> ' . . . the Union's objective shall be to provide citizens with a high level of safety within an area of freedom, security and justice by developing common action among the Member States in the fields of police and judicial co-operation in criminal matters and by preventing and combating racism and xenophobia.'
>
> *Article 29, The Amsterdam Treaty*

Europol is already developing a state of the art computer analysis system, operational in 2001, which is accessible *only* to Europol analysts. Excluding the staff, it costs about £7 million ($11 million) a year to run and develop. The raw data is quite reasonably only available to the country that submitted it. But Europol officers use that data to create analyses. Only Europol officers have full access at will to those analyses. The British police or other national police forces do not.

Europol is building files on individuals who are criminals, suspects, witnesses and potential sources which can include just about anybody. Each entry in the database has 56 fields including ethnic origins, sexuality, and political and religious views. That should alarm everyone especially given the EU Race Directive, its track record on Austria and the proposals to ban political parties see page 261.

Under the Amsterdam Treaty, ratified in May 1999,

Europol took a leap forward. The Treaty effectively gave Europol the authority to move from simple co-operation between independent police forces towards a new European authority. The Treaty terms, which should come fully into operation by May 2004, included,

○ Expanding Europol's remit and police co-operation from serious crime to all crime, 'organised or otherwise' and 'by preventing racism and xenophobia.' No further mention was made in that treaty of racism and xenophobia and especially how they might be defined.

○ Europol, through its local national unit, can ask the British police to investigate individuals and crimes in Britain. At present the British police can refuse and they need not give any reasons. Like so many areas of the EU, in practice the British police will probably try to co-operate. That may make it more difficult to refuse in the future.

○ Europol officers can take part in joint operations anywhere in the EU including Britain in a 'support capacity' in a joint investigation team.

Joint Investigation Teams

What 'joint teams' means is still not clear.

The plan agreed by all the EU countries at the 1999 Tampere Summit was for,

> 'joint investigative teams . . . to be set up without delay, as a first step, to combat trafficking in drugs and human beings as well as terrorism . . . The rules to be set up in this respect should allow Europol to participate, as appropriate, in such teams in a support capacity.'
>
> *Recommendation 43, October 1999*

The European Police Office

Europol's Mission Statement

Europol is the European Law Enforcement Organisation, which aims at improving the effectiveness and co-operation of the competent authorities in the Member States in preventing and combating terrorism, unlawful drug trafficking and other forms of serious international organised crime. The mission of Europol is to make a significant contribution to the European Union's law enforcement action against organised crime with a particular emphasis on the criminal organisations involved.

The Europol web site at www.eupol.eu.int

Both Europol and European police, for example French or German or Spanish police, would have a greater role in criminal investigations in Britain or any other EU country.

The 'support' those police would give to investigations according to a European Council Recommendation was,

○ Europol's knowledge of the criminal world
○ Help in co-ordinating operations
○ Technical support
○ Help in analysing offences

The Commission did not think that went far enough. At the last minute it included Joint Teams in a Convention reaching the end of lengthy negotiations (see page 46 *The Convention On Mutual Assistance In Criminal Matters*). Britain agreed to the Convention in May 2000.

The revised Convention says that a representative of the country in which the joint team operates would be the team leader but police from other Member States could be seconded to the team. Seconded officers could take 'certain investigative measures', subject to the approval of the country of operation and their own country.

The British government agreed that the Convention went further than previous agreements because,

> '[It conferred] a potential power of intervention on officers seconded to a joint team operating in another Member State.'

The government pointed out that seconded officers would only be able to take action with the agreement of the Member State of operation and 'the Government did not intend to confer any such powers in the UK.' The government had long held that,

> 'Europol staff should not have operational powers

and that any involvement in criminal investigations by joint teams should take the form of analytical and expert support.'

House of Lords Select Committee on the EC 12th Report,
18.7.2000

Because a Europol officer's role in a joint team would be 'the traditional one of analysis' they would not even need to be present on British territory. The government failed to mention that Europol officers are already in Britain where they have a local office.

Although the government said that Europol officers and other EU police should not operate in Britain in joint teams, the thrust of the Amsterdam Treaty and the Convention is that they should, if not today then soon.

It is likely that the Commission will find an opportunity to ensure that both Europol and European police can operate in Britain and not remain behind their desks.

The EU Police College

A top EU priority is an EU police college. The more courses are held the more the college could advance the cause of creating a unified EU police force by 'educating' police officers to 'think European'.

Europol already runs inter-service courses for police officers at the European Police College at Leusden in the Netherlands. Under the Amsterdam Treaty Europol, as well as other EU police forces were encouraged to co-operate on training, equipment and forensic research as well as exchanging officers and arranging secondments. The EU now plans its own staff college, like the British Police Staff College at Bramshill in Hampshire. It will be done in two stages.

Stage one, close to fruition, uses the existing national staff colleges to run EU courses for senior officers. Police from countries about to join the EU, such as Poland and the Czech Republic, will also be able to take part. The outside of the buildings will look the same as ever to anyone passing by but part of the content will have changed. It is hollowing out from within. The secretariat for these courses will probably be somewhere in Britain.

Stage two would be a European Police Staff College with its own headquarters and secretariat. The EU says that in the longer term merely networking the police colleges, including those of candidate countries, cannot be an adequate solution. At present some police schools, such as the Budapest Police Institute, employ American teachers who, according to Brussels, would not be welcome in the EU.

Europol In The Eyes Of Its Chief

Jorgen Storbeck, the German police officer running Europol, has constantly campaigned for more powers and consistently emphasised the threat of serious crime in an EU without borders.

On 21st September 1999, Storbeck gave a speech to the British Police Federation. He stated,

> 'Despite radical changes, sovereignty remains deeply ingrained . . . as far as internal security is concerned.
>
> 'No-one would argue about the supremacy of law but . . . we can, and must, be more flexible in relation to who enforces it. The difficulties encountered in international police co-operation stem from this attachment to sovereignty in law enforcement.'
>
> Europol will 'stand or fall according to whether Member States supply [it with] good quality infor-

mation . . . The signs are mixed at present. If they do not, then we have to go and find it, then the calls for Europol to have executive powers may prove irresistible.'

Just like the Roman Empire the EU is proposing to break national ties by posting police officers from one country to another: an Italian to Britain, a Briton to France and so on, operating in a multinational force under one command. This breaking of national ties has already started in a completely different area – inspectors of slaughterhouses (see page 212).

Europol In The Future

Among EU proposals yet to be agreed by Member States are,

o Europol should be under the control of a Commissioner. Europol would then be an EU police force carrying out the wishes of the Commission. The link with Member States would be broken. A management board on which each Member State is represented today runs Europol; the Director General of the NCIS represents Britain.

o The European Public Prosecutor 'independent of national governments and Community institutions' and 'accountable to no-one', should supervise all Europol investigations. The continental practice is that the police are not responsible for investigating a crime. All investigations are started and supervised by a judge under the overall authority of the Public Prosecutor. The police are merely his agents.

House of Lords Select Committee on European Communities 9th Report 'Prosecuting Fraud On The Communities' Finances— The Corpus Juris', 18.5.1999

○ Eurojust, the half way house to a European Public Prosecutor, will from 2001 help to co-ordinate national prosecuting authorities and support criminal investigations into organised crime cases based on Europol's analysis.

An EU Police Reaction Unit Or A Riot Police?

In June 2000 the EU Member States agreed that by 2003 they would provide up to 5,000 police officers for international missions. Up to 1,000 police officers within 30 days could be deployed. The British government has enthusiastically backed the plans for the Police Reaction Unit.

The Police Reaction Unit would not be used inside the EU. It would not be a riot police, said the EU.

Operations will be led either by the UN (or other international agency) or the EU, but not by Britain or any other national government. The police will be organised in integrated units of officers from the different EU countries, and nearly all will be armed.

Missions could range from conflict prevention to crisis management, to preventing internal conflicts and 'restoring law and order' all over the world, for example Kosovo, East Timor and El Salvador. Police from other countries have long been used to restore order in war torn areas like Kosovo. 3,300 police from EU Member States are already serving round the world in international missions but they are responsible to their national police forces.

The Police Reaction Unit has been on the EU agenda for some time but progress was slow. Like the EU's army, the war in Kosovo provided the impetus and the excuse to accelerate this programme. An EU Committee for Civilian Aspects of Crisis Management held its first meeting in June 2000. It has,

o A database of EU countries' police capabilities and shares information
o A liaison office, linked to the EU Commission, at the European Council Secretariat
o Targets for a 'collective' non-military response, including civilian policing, humanitarian aid, administrative and legal rehabilitation, search, and rescue, electoral and human rights monitoring

The EU intends the Police Reaction Unit should help to

o Prevent the start or escalation of conflicts
o Reinforce internal stability in transitional periods
o Work with the EU armed forces in the full range of Petersberg tasks (see page 88)

But this EU police force could one day be used within Member States to restore order though there are no spoken plans to do so.

Article 297 of the Treaty of Rome states,

'Member States shall consult one another with a view to taking together the steps needed to prevent the functioning of the common market being affected by measures which a Member State may be called upon to take in the event of serious internal disturbances affecting the maintenance of law and order, in the event of war, serious international tension constituting a threat of war, or in order to carry out obligations it has accepted for the purpose of maintaining peace and international security.'

This clause could easily be amended enabling the EU Police

Reaction Unit to operate *within* the borders of the EU to maintain law and order EU style, ostensibly to 'keep the single market functioning'.

An EU Mobile Government

A mobile government will accompany the crisis police to countries where the administration has collapsed. It will give,

- Aid to re-establish a judicial and penal system including national plans to select and train judges, prosecutors, and penal experts and deploy them at short notice
- Guidelines to select and train international judges and penal experts in liaison with the UN
- Support to establish or rebuild local courts and prisons, as well as recruit local personnel to back peace operations

The EU says its mobile government could be used in natural disasters under the umbrella of the EU's Common Foreign and Security Policy.

How Close Is A Police State?

When the EU expands to the East and South-east from 2006 onwards, a central police force may be the key to holding the disparate former countries together and to ensure the central will is imposed on them all. And as EU policies become ever more apparent to people in the present EU countries the central police force and the Police Reaction Unit may be essential to maintain Brussels' law and Brussels' order. Will the British government agree to it? Will it have a choice?

Chapter 6

EIN REICH, EIN VOLK, EIN WEHRMACHT

Giving Up Britain's Secure Defence, Undermining NATO,
Jeopardising Britain's Defence Industries and 400,000 Jobs

All the armed forces of all the federated nations will become a single force, owing allegiance to the federal government and not to the national governments. There will be no British Navy, no German army, no French air force, but British, German, French, Swedish, Belgian . . . contingents of a federal navy, army and air force.

From a European constitution proposed by
the Fabian Society in 1940

NATO has kept the peace in Europe for 50 years. The North Atlantic Treaty, signed in 1949, created a defensive alliance of 12 independent countries including the Americans. The heart of the alliance is Article 5, 'an armed attack against one is an attack against all.'

Yet today the Blair government is undermining the NATO alliance, creating a rift with the US, joining with under funded and often indifferently trained European armies in a unified army speaking several languages, to pursue a foreign policy which is unlikely to be in Britain's national interest and for which British troops may be asked to put their lives at risk.

Britain has already said yes to the first stages of EU defence procurement, which is likely to damage Britain's highly successful defence industries and its world-class research and development.

First Plans For European Defence

'Some of them had let us down. Some of them had fought against us. All of them were seen in 1948 to be liable to communist intervention.'

Lord Garner on Britain's wartime European allies

'A European army would be a sludgy amalgam.'

Winston Churchill

When North Korea invaded South Korea on 25th June 1950, President Truman increased the American army fast and sent extra troops to Europe in case the Russians surged westward. Truman planned to create ten German divisions under NATO command. Only five years after the end of the Second World War the idea of German divisions rang alarm bells in France. François Quilici said in a National Assembly debate,

'The Americans will leave one day. But they will have re-created and developed German power over our frontier . . . the story, the sad story, is beginning again.'

Jean Monnet, unelected president of the new European Coal and Steel Community, feared his organisation might not survive the Korean crisis and proposed adding a defence arm, a European Defence Community, with a European Defence Minister responsible to the Council of Ministers and a Common Assembly. German soldiers in the new army would wear a European uniform.

'The federation of Europe would have to become an immediate objective. The army . . . [would] have to be placed . . . under joint sovereignty. *We could no longer wait, as we had once planned*, for political Europe to be the culminating point of a gradual process, since its joint defence was inconceivable without a joint political authority . . . '

France And Germany, The Crucial Axis, And The Treaty of Elysée

The German question has dominated European politics since the defeat of Napoleon.

In January 1963, seven years after regaining sovereignty and international respectability, Germany signed a Treaty of Reconciliation with France, the Treaty of Elysée. That treaty was of crucial importance to the future of European union. When he signed it President de Gaulle firmly turned his back on Britain and on Harold Macmillan's request to join the EEC. He did so because of Britain's close relationship, especially a military one, with the US.

Just before signing the treaty, de Gaulle and Germany's Chancellor Adenauer knelt together before the High Altar of Rheims Cathedral and reviewed troops on the fields of Charlemagne, symbolically saluting the European ideal. The two leaders differed in their view of *Europe*. De Gaulle opposed German ambitions for a united Europe; he wanted a Europe of nation states but his dream was to die with him.

As the Elysée Treaty guaranteed, the German and French heads of state, the German and French Ministers of Foreign Affairs, and those responsible for defence and for youth have since met twice every year. Those meetings have proved to be the driving force towards a united Europe. So many initiatives have first been agreed between the French and the Germans and then endorsed by the rest of the EU.

Over nearly 40 years and despite occasional differences of view a gradual build up of cultural exchanges, youth parliaments, substantial exchanges between the two civil services, and joint colleges has led, as intended, to an ever closer union.

Together, France and Germany have blazed the way to an EU army as they have in all areas of EU policy. But until the

Berlin Wall fell and the Soviet threat from across the border to the east lessened, Germany's first loyalty was to the US, its military protector, and therefore to NATO.

Meanwhile France, protected from the Soviet threat by NATO and the buffer of Germany, could afford to indulge in its traditional anti-Americanism and withdraw from NATO in 1966. All the time, France was trying to control Germany's political ambitions.

An EU Foreign And Defence Policy – The History

> The Heads of Government decided to 'transform, before the end of the decade . . . the whole complex of the relations of member states into a European Union.'
>
> *Paris Summit Conclusions, October 1972*

1970 – Led by Edward Heath, Willy Brandt and Georges Pompidou for Britain, West Germany and France, the original Six agreed to begin European Political Co-operation. That meant regular meetings between the Foreign Ministers and the diplomatic services of the EEC members to discuss a joint foreign policy.

1973 – The member states stepped up the rate of diplomatic meetings to seek common approaches and put them into practice. Foreign policy still remained outside the treaties, with no formal structure.

1973/4 – The project was set back by a decade when the price of oil rose dramatically and the world economy fell into recession.

1983 – The small steps to a unified country began again, and the informal dialogue on foreign policy now included the political and economic aspects of security, but not yet the armed forces themselves.

1984 – All the Foreign and Defence Ministers of the Western European Union (WEU), now the acknowledged vehicle to create a European defence force, declared they wanted a European security identity and gradually to 'harmonise' their defence policies. The WEU agreed to hold two meetings a year for Foreign and Defence Ministers at the same conference table. The reactivated WEU liaised between NATO and the EU.

The Western European Union (WEU)

The WEU is a self-defence group of some European countries. The Brussels Treaty created it in 1948, when fear of the Soviet Union was increasing rapidly.

When NATO was formed only a year later in 1949, bringing in the Americans and Canadians, the WEU's role became nominal.

The WEU does not have the same membership as the EU. While the 10 WEU countries are all NATO allies, the EU includes non-NATO countries and neutrals.

1986 – For the first time foreign policy was brought within the treaties in the Single European Act, although it remained subject to the national veto. It was to be reviewed in 1991. The EU Commission was now 'fully associated' with foreign policy. The member states agreed to

○ 'ensure that common principles and objectives are gradually developed and defined' and so advance to one foreign policy
○ The President of the Commission was to initiate action, co-ordinate and represent member states, backed up by a secretariat in Brussels with diplomatic status

Far too late, and 23 years after the Treaty of Elysée, Margaret Thatcher, the British Prime Minister, realised, as she later wrote in her memoirs *The Downing Street Years*, 'A Franco-German bloc with its own agenda had re-emerged to set the direction of the Community.'

1987 – Negotiations between the US and the USSR on the withdrawal of intermediate nuclear forces gave greater security to the West and the opportunity for the then EEC to take another step towards one army.

The WEU countries agreed on a report, *The Hague Platform*, which set out guidelines to 'strengthen the European pillar of the (Atlantic) Alliance.' The preamble said

> 'We are convinced that the construction of an integrated Europe will remain incomplete as long as it does not include security and defence.'

1987 and 1988 – France and German agreed a number of firsts at their regular meetings,

○ French and German officers to hold seminars at the military school in Paris
○ Joint military exercises of 75,000 men in Germany
○ A Franco-German defence council
○ The two countries to build a military helicopter together
○ A Franco-German defence college
○ A Franco-German brigade of 5,000 men based in Strasbourg

The WEU had never had a serious defence role. Now minesweepers from EU countries, flying the WEU flag, helped to clear the Straits of Hormuz of mines at the end of the Iran-Iraq war.

The Berlin Wall Falls And European Defence Begins In Earnest

> 'A united Europe without a common defence is, in the long run, not feasible.'
>
> *Chancellor Kohl of Germany*

On 9th November 1989 the Berlin Wall was torn down. Within the year the two Germanys were reunited. By the end of 1991 the Soviet Empire had broken up and all western countries slashed their defence budgets.

For the first time for 50 years Germany was no longer under threat from the East and it began to break away from American protection. Germany reverted to Bismarck's policy of friendship with Russia, and a deep concern with its eastern borders and the Balkans. Germany now used the umbrella of the EU to legitimise its aims in Central and Eastern Europe.

Three years after the fall of the Berlin Wall the 1992 Maastricht Treaty reflected the dramatically changed European picture.

For the first time the Commission in Brussels was at least as important as the member states on foreign policy, which became known as the Common Foreign and Security Policy or CFSP.

- The Commission had the right to set policy jointly with the member states
- States could still take individual action *provided* they kept to EC objectives
- 'The member States shall support the union's external and security policy actively and unreservedly . . . they shall refrain from any action which is contrary to the interests of the Union . . . ' said the treaty

For the first time defence was explicitly mentioned. The treaty said,

'The common foreign and security policy shall
include all questions related to the security of the
Union, including the eventual framing of a common
defence policy, which might in time lead to a common defence, thereby reinforcing the European
identity and its independence . . . The union shall
request the WEU, which is an integral part of the
development of the European Union, to elaborate
and implement decisions and actions of the Union
which have defence implications . . . respect(ing)
the obligations of certain Member states under
NATO.'

The neutral EU countries, Austria, Ireland and Sweden,
which are not members of the WEU, could either join or
observe.

At their 59th Summit in 1992, France and Germany agreed
to upgrade the Franco-German brigade to an army corps,
called Eurocorps, open to new members, and operating under
EU instruction via the WEU. At first French and German
troops made up the 50,000 strong corps and today it includes
forces from Belgium, Luxembourg, the Netherlands and
Spain. Its remit is to operate within Article V of the WEU and
Article 5 of NATO.

The Americans Become Alarmed

The Americans made their position clear in a telegram sent to
all EC and NATO countries while the WEU was meeting in
March 1991. It became known as the Bartholomew Telegram
after its sender, the US Under-Secretary of Defence Reginald
Bartholomew.

The Americans were prepared to encourage a European
voice within NATO, but with limits,

○ No European caucus inside NATO
○ No marginalisation of non-EC members of NATO
○ No alternative defence organisation for Europeans

The End Of National Diplomacy And The Rise Of The Uniform External Service

> 'The Treaty of Amsterdam . . . is the continuation of the political project set in motion in the 50s. It reinforces the Treaty of Maastricht in many aspects but its main features can be seen in CFSP.'
>
> *Elmar Brok MEP, Chairman of EU Parliament's Committee on Foreign Affairs, Human Rights, Common Security, and Defence policy in testimony to the US Congress, November 1999*

The Amsterdam Treaty, ratified in 1999, strengthened the EU even more and weakened the nation states.

○ Now the EU *alone*, not the member states, defined and executed the CFSP
○ National policies *had* to agree with the EU position
○ Joint actions could *only* be taken by qualified majority voting with no national veto
○ Now the Common Foreign and Security Policy included *everything* on the security of the EU 'including the progressive framing of a common defence policy'
○ The WEU was to be integrated into the EU

A Mr. CFSP, in EU jargon, was appointed.

By the time of the Amsterdam Treaty most areas of British foreign policy making had already moved to Brussels, where the British diplomats joined 28 EU working groups to decide so-called 'common positions'. Each EU committee has two British representatives, one London based and one from Britain's diplomatic representation to the EU.

British foreign policy has become so Brussels orientated that ambitious British diplomats seek EU postings or the EU desks in London to further their careers. The rest of the world has been correspondingly downgraded.

Carefully drafted diplomatic answers full of evasion and half-truths are routinely given to anyone questioning the trend of 'British' foreign policy.

That trend does not reflect Britain's trade interests, which are truly global.

Pioneered as usual by France and Germany, exchanges of diplomatic staff between member states are now routine. In the first half of 2000 there were two Germans and one Frenchman on secondment for a year in the Foreign Office in London, with British diplomats working in the Foreign Ministries of Portugal, Holland and Germany.

Foreign nationals within the British Foreign Office have certainly created security problems, though not so far insuperable ones for the intelligence services. They have had to limit the circulation of sensitive material, which has sounded an alarm with Britain's allies across the Atlantic. As EU foreign policy becomes ever more integrated there will be a deepening wedge between Britain and its NATO allies, the US and Canada.

No longer are British issues of foreign policy decided exclusively in London. The Brussels working group system is all-powerful and is reflected in press releases. When President Mugabe's campaign of violence in Zimbabwe threatened the security of 20,000 British citizens, the evacuation plan was labelled as an EU plan and it was formulated in Brussels.

The EU has 132 embassies round the world though it calls them delegations. Officially the EU is not yet a sovereign state, because it does not have legal identity yet.

The EU heads of delegations are already ambassadors in all

but name. They present letters of credence to the local heads of state and are treated as part of the local diplomatic corps with the glamour and expense accounts to go with it. The 'ambassadors' drive out from their official residencies in official cars, flying the EU flag.

With huge overseas aid money to dispense, including a quarter of Britain's aid budget of over £800 million a year ($1.2 billion), the 'ambassadors' have clout. EU diplomats are now organised in a Uniform External Service.

They cannot yet issue passports or look after EU 'citizens', or defence matters but all that is just a matter of time and EU legal identity.

When in April 2000 the German Finance Minister, Hans Eichel, suggested that EU members abolish their embassies in each other's countries and run joint embassies in other countries there was a flurry of furious rebuffs from round the EU.

Only five months later, in September 2000, the EU Parliament approved a plan for a fully-fledged foreign service, with its own embassies around the world and an elite training academy.

British, French and German embassies would be gradually merged and the EU would take responsibility for running foreign policy.

On international bodies such as the UN where Britain and France separately have seats on the Security Council, the IMF and the World Bank there would be what the EU euphemistically calls 'co-ordinated representation'.

Once that plan is put into operation Britain will not be able to operate as a sovereign country anywhere in the world. Operations in the Gulf, in the Falklands or backing Britain's trade interests will be impossible.

The EU is deadly serious about running Britain's foreign policy and there is no serious British opposition to it.

EU foreign policy is already truly global. For example, at a conference in Rio de Janeiro in June 1999 proposals to create an EU customs union with Latin America were debated.

The EU sees itself as a rival to the US on the world stage.

EU Defence Policy In The 1990s – A Steady Advance

> 'The Franco-German relationship is intimately and irreversibly enmeshed in the European project. The European project's greatest achievement is the reconciliation of France and Germany. In turn the European project would not be where it is without the Franco-German push.'
>
> *Ambassador Bujon de l'Estang at Harvard University,*
>
> *14.4.1997*

The Bosnian crisis gave the excuse and impetus for the Foreign and Defence Ministers of the WEU to promote a new defence role. The Ministers met in June 1992 at Petersberg, near Bonn, to agree what became known as the Petersberg tasks,

- o Humanitarian and rescue missions
- o Peacekeeping
- o Crisis management

To prepare to carry out their self-appointed Petersberg tasks the WEU countries agreed,

- o The WEU Chiefs of Defence staff, Britain included, meet twice each year
- o Military delegates were now part of all national delegations
- o Brussels was the new headquarters of EU defence and the WEU council and secretariat was moved from London to Brussels

○ A planning cell began to prepare contingency plans and recommendations for command and control and communications arrangements

Despite all the planning there was no army to carry out the Petersberg tasks. And those tasks have yet to be clearly defined; it is a truly murky area. Even eight years later they remained unclear. The House of Lords noted that,

'The Petersberg tasks cover a wide range of missions. At one end of the scale, they include peace-making, which can include war fighting.'

Para. 99 15th Report 'The Common European Policy On Security And Defence', 25.7.2000

The geographical limits of EU intervention are equally murky and the witnesses to the same House of Lords Select Committee offered no agreement, much speculation and talk of decisions to be made on a case by case basis. The Committee itself assumed that Bosnia and Kososvo type operations were quite likely and even UN-led missions in Somalia, Rwanda, Burundi, East Timor and Sierra Leone. The Lords commented,

'Surprisingly, a scenario like Rwanda was seen as particularly appropriate for EU involvement by Mr Richard Hatfield, Policy Director of the Ministry of Defence. He told us that *were that situation to come up again, it could be done under European Union auspices but it would not be done under NATO auspices because NATO has no security role in relation to Central Africa.* A UN mandate for this type of operation would be important in shaping the character of such deployments both inside and outside Europe.'

France And Germany Spearhead The Drive To An EU Army, Foreign Policy And Everything Else

1992	Eurocorps, the European army corps, created
	Eurocorps established in Strasbourg with 40,000 French and German soldiers, 10,000 from Belgium, Spain and Luxembourg and 1,000 HQ staff
	First permanent Franco-German foreign affairs committee to develop 'political co-operation'
	French and German Ambassadors conference relaunched to co-ordinate policies in Eastern Europe
	French and German navies to exchange young officers
1994	200 German soldiers marched down the Champs Elysées on Bastille Day
1995	The French and German Ministries of Foreign Affairs held first twice-yearly seminar
1996	Conference of French and German ambassadors held in Berlin on Russia and the Ukraine – the eastern border of the EU
	President Chirac of France backed Germany's demand for a seat on the UN Security Council
	German soldiers formed the first French-German brigade and went to Bosnia–Herzegovina
	President Chirac said France needed the six years after the Cold War 'to construct a credible European defence, capable of becoming both the armed wing of the EU and the European pillar of the Atlantic Alliance'
1997	Members of the German Bundesrat and the French Senate held first working parties
	Exchanges agreed between the French and German embassies
	French-German University at Saarbrucken agreed

In July 1998 the first Eurocorps troops joined SFOR in Bosnia. The EU army was now marching outside its own borders.

The US Continues To Back The EU

The US supported the EU's growing efforts to create a European Security and Defence Identity (ESDI) *within* NATO, while hoping that the Europeans would make a greater practical contribution to NATO.

1994 – The Americans backed the NATO launch of the Combined Joint Task Force (CJTF) to allow limited autonomy to European forces. Forces for European only missions could be detached by either NATO or the WEU, and backed by American materiel and logistics. But the Americans would still be in control.

1996 – NATO defence and foreign ministers approved the new CJFT command arrangements for WEU-led operations giving a key role to the Deputy Supreme Commander (DSSACEUR), always a European. This was expressly to allow an ESDI within NATO.

The EU Is Not Facing Reality

'There is an agenda being advanced in Europe regardless of the threat.'
Iain Duncan-Smith, British Shadow Defence Secretary, to a US Congressional Committee, 10.11.1999

Possible threats to NATO countries range from regional conflicts involving countries with strong commercial and strategic links with the west to the proliferation of biological, chemical, and nuclear weapons. The Rumsfeld Report to the

US Congress in July 1998 forecast that within five years rogue states in Asia, Middle East and North Africa could have the ability to strike the nations of Europe and the US. Alarmed, the US began an anti-ballistic missile programme.

The EU is not even discussing the possible threats to which it would have to match its defence. In January 2000 Britain reverted to its old trans-Atlantic role and asked the Americans for a share in the anti-ballistic umbrella, and offered to broker discussions with the EU.

EU assets are pitiful.

In the 1999 Kosovo conflict the Americans provided almost three-quarters of the aircraft, more than four fifths of the bombs and most of the intelligence. The EU countries had two million men under arms, yet only the British could get more than two per cent of their troops to Kosovo.

The combined EU defence budget is about half the Americans' budget of $290 billion. Spending on military R&D is a quarter of US spending. Weapons procurement is plagued by lack of funds, under performance, delays and cost over-runs.

European forces have no airborne tanks, no long-range missiles, no precision guided missiles, and only one French military reconnaissance satellite. The EU lacks intelligence gathering, strategic airlift, and command and control.

The EU cannot yet fight a war alone but the Kosovan conflict has reinforced the drive to create a European army.

John R. Bolton of the American Enterprise Institute in his evidence to the US Congress in November 1999 said that 'Blair's *hawkishness* (in Kosovo) was . . . a classic *free ride*, both politically and militarily. He knew that President Clinton would accept a ground war only with the greatest reluctance, and he also knew that American troops, technology and support would be central to any NATO ground effort.'

German Vital Interests Are Paramount

'EU enlargement is a supreme national interest, especially for Germany.'

Joschka Fischer, German Foreign Minister, speech at the
Humboldt University, Berlin, 12.5.2000

Ignoring global threats, which it cannot in any case hope to address, the EU is concentrating on local interests, or rather local to Germany. They are the traditional German border interests to the East and Southeast. They are not traditional NATO interests although NATO has gone along with them.

The EU has 'common' strategies towards Russia, Ukraine, and the West Balkans. Most of those strategies are marginal to British interests. Some of those strategies are grandiose pretensions.

Federal Trust, a leading pro-EU British think tank, claimed in a paper *Security of the Union* in October 1995 that,

'(the EU) has a responsibility for ensuring the future security and stability of the European continent . . . to create stability in Central and Eastern Europe without pushing Russia into a complex of insecurity with all the danger of the Cold War . . . ultimately European security is about incorporating Russia into a European security system . . . '

Germany has been prominent in the 'solutions' in the Balkans reflecting the strength of German concern. For example, in 1999 Tom Keonig assumed operational control of Kosovo reporting to a UN special representative. His brief included policing, creating a judicial system and integrating the KLA into the government. Bodo Hombach runs the EU Stability Pact for the whole of Balkans and a German general commanded KFOR from autumn 1999.

At the time of the NATO attacks on Kosovo it was widely alleged that the war would further the cause of European integration. It was no surprise, therefore, that Eurocorps took over the running of the KFOR intervention force.

The EU Stability Pact for South Eastern Europe aims to incorporate the whole area into the EU. A similar stability pact has been proposed for the Caucasus.

Labour Betrays The British Armed Forces

If the EU is to have its own army, Britain and France are the keys to it. Britain and France are the only two European permanent members of the UN Security Council. They are the only EU countries with nuclear capability. They are the only EU countries able to project military force rapidly beyond their own borders.

Britain has always been a strong supporter of NATO and the Americans. Just as Churchill recognised that Nazi Germany could never be defeated without the US, every Prime Minister since then has understood the importance of NATO and especially of the American forces.

Tony Blair's Labour government ignored sixty years of experience. Blair's policy endangered the British armed forces and Britain's special relationship with the US. He embraced a chimera because there was no substance to EU defence, it was largely talk. Blair probably wanted to project a 'good European' image to the rest of the EU while maintaining a strong Atlantic link. He was trying the circus act of riding two horses at once, but the two horses were going in opposite directions.

At an informal EU Summit at Portschach in October 1998

Tony Blair told a press conference that 'Europe should be able to play a better, more *unified* part in foreign and security policy decision.' He later added,

> 'A common foreign and security policy for the European Union is necessary, it is overdue, it is needed and it is high time we got on with it . . . '

Blair qualified that with the familiar chorus 'we need to make sure that the institutional mechanism in no way undermines NATO . . . '

Blair's position was criticised in the House of Commons, by the Tory MP Crispin Blunt, who commented,

> 'In the long term, this would mean the establishment of something akin to a European Foreign and Defence Ministry.'

John Spellar, Labour's Defence under-secretary, replied,

> 'Our aim is to strengthen Europe's position in the world . . . We want to ensure that Europe can speak with authority and act with decisiveness . . . it requires the establishment of an effective defence capability . . . '

Spellar notably did not say that the Labour government wished to strengthen Britain's position in the world and the effectiveness of Britain's defence capability.

At NATO's Edinburgh meeting in November 1998, Tony Blair proclaimed,

> 'Europe needs genuine military operational capability – not least forces able to react quickly and work together effectively – and genuine political will . . . we want a new debate. Our US allies have often called for more burden sharing. They have not

always been keen to see a greater European identity of view . . .'

To look good in the EU Blair was prepared to ignore the realities of power politics and vital British interests and give the Franco-German axis under the guise of the EU the leverage to move swiftly to one defence force subsuming Britain's armed forces.

In December 1998 Tony Blair met President Chirac of France at St Malo and turned his back on NATO. Their agreement appeared to be of minor importance: co-operation such as posting liaison officers to operational headquarters, attaching two ships to the French Carrier task group, and joint exercises.

In fact it was a major break as the joint Blair-Chirac statement shows,

> 'The EU needs to be [able] to play its full role on the international stage . . . the Union must have the capacity for *autonomous* action, backed up by credible military forces, the means to decide to use them, and a readiness to do so in order to respond to international crises . . . The EU will also need to have recourse to suitable military means . . . within NATO's European pillar or . . . means *outside the NATO framework.*'

The French said this was a major step towards the creation of 'an autonomous European defence system to emerge in the long run . . . [to] take place within the framework of the CFSP.' The French were right.

Britain was rapidly moving towards acknowledging French, and therefore German, leadership of European defence.

The German Defence Minister, Rudolf Scharping, wrote in *Die Zeit* on 18th February 1999,

'With the initiative by Prime Minster Blair in Portschach on 3-4th November 1998, the Franco-German Summit statement in Potsdam on 1st December and the Franco-British statement of St Malo on 4th December 1998, the prospects for speeding up the process of European integration have decisively improved.'

The Spanish Foreign Minister, Abel Matutes, in a Spanish radio interview on 8th December 1998 said,

'[the agreement is a] new openness from Britain . . . what Britain is doing is clearing the way for this idea, the integration of the WEU into the EU, the majority of we European states have been close to achieving it.'

In merging the WEU with the EU Britain ignored its previous qualms about the neutral status of four EU members, Austria, Finland, Ireland and Sweden. France and Germany, the protagonists of an EU army, had always ignored the neutrality issue. Despite their neutrality the Finnish and Swedish governments welcomed the St Malo agreement provided that it related to crisis management and not mutual defence.

Blair repeated his usual chorus to the British Parliament on 14th December,

'There is of course no question of undermining NATO in any way. Strengthening the European defence capability will strengthen NATO.'

William Hague for the Conservatives challenged that,

'Where are the Prime Minster's guiding principles on Europe? What has happened to his defence policy? The Labour Party manifesto states *Our*

security will continue to be based on NATO.
Following the Amsterdam Summit, the Prime
Minister described proposals along precisely the
lines now being suggested as, *an ill judged Franco-
German transplant operation.* Why has he changed
his mind so dramatically? Do not the proposals in
fact endanger our commitment to NATO?'

George Robertson, the British Defence Secretary, reassured
the Americans that,

'[there is] no question of a European single army; no
[EU] Commission or European Parliament involvement in decision making; no transfer of decision
making on military capability from individual
Governments; and no undermining or duplication
of NATO.'

Madeleine Albright, the US Secretary of State, welcomed
any agreement to help burden sharing but warned against
Europeans duplicating military structures such as forces and
headquarters with NATO.

The former American ambassador to NATO, Robert
Hunter, hit the nail on the head when he called the St Malo
agreement,

'short on substance but long on political significance.'

Jane's Defence Weekly, 3.3.1999

'A new step in the construction of the EU'

Tony Blair gave the green light and Germany rapidly pushed
through an agenda for an EU army during 1999 ready for the
next EU Treaty to be signed at Nice in December 2000.

In March 1999 Germany proposed to an informal EU Foreign Ministers meeting that not only should the EU be able to lead operations using NATO assets (and that meant mainly American assets), but the EU should lead operations, mainly for crisis management, *without* recourse to NATO assets.

At the April 50th anniversary NATO Summit in Washington the alliance agreed to make its military assets available 'for use in EU-led operations' such as peace keeping or humanitarian relief which should be 'further developed'. DSACEUR (NATO's deputy commander, always a European) was to be Mr. EU Defence.

Critically, while the EU gained direct access to NATO assets, the US still controlled any EU operation. President Clinton said,

> 'As long as this operation, however it is constituted by the Europeans, operates in co-operation with NATO, I think it will strengthen the capability of the alliance, and I think it will actually help to maintain America's involvement with NATO.'

William Hague questioned in the Commons where the EU-led capability would leave countries of vital strategic importance such as Turkey, a NATO member but outside the EU,

> 'The [NATO] communiqué says that the European defence identity will be developed within the NATO structures but the St Malo agreement provided for the development of an EU defence inside or outside NATO. Are these two agreements reconciled easily?'

In May 1999, France and Germany agreed to,

○ Secure those non-American assets
○ Integrate the WEU into the EU
○ Turn the Eurocorps of 60,000 men into a European Rapid Reaction Corps with naval and air combat elements
○ At the latest by 2003, the Corps will have 120,000 to 150,000 men, 'separable from NATO but not separate', 300 to 500 aircraft (roughly half to be combat aircraft) and 15 large combat ships

France and Germany said that the European Rapid Reaction Corps would be able to undertake the most demanding crisis management tasks in more than one place at once, with the possibility of long-term interventions. It would deploy in full at corps level (up to 15 brigades or 50,000 to 60,000 men) within 60 days while providing a smaller force at very high readiness. The main force should be capable of deployment for at least one year. A force of over 200,000 men would be needed to field the 15 brigades.

In June 1999 the EU Cologne Summit endorsed the Franco-German agenda. Stung by the disparities between US and EU military capabilities exposed by the Kosovan war, the EU countries agreed a December 2000 deadline for more independent action 'backed up by credible military forces, the means to use them and the readiness to do so'. 'We are now determined to launch a new step in the construction of the European Union', said the Presidency conclusions.

Javier Solana, the retiring secretary general of NATO, became the first secretary general for CFSP (Mr. CSFP) with a strategic planning and an early warning unit reporting to him. His job was to provide united policies, give them a higher profile, and convince the rest of the world that the EU meant business on defence issues. When Washington calls he is at the end of the telephone representing the EU.

The EU still repeated the usual chorus, 'The [NATO] Alliance remains the foundation of the collective defence of its member States.' That refrain was sounding more and more hollow with each repetition.

The Cologne and Helsinki Decisions
June and December 1999

- Endorsement of the Franco-German agreement for the European Rapid Reaction Corps
- Regular meetings of the General Affairs council, including Defence Ministers. The 15 defence ministers met together for the first time at the Helsinki Summit
- A standing Political and Security Committee (PSC) in Brussels of national representatives of ambassador level to deal with all aspects of the CFSP including defence. In a crisis this committee will control the political and strategic direction of the operation sending guidelines to the military committee. It is still tied to nation states because it reports to the Council of Ministers. Brussels describes this as 'an interim committee' because of its national links
- Military Committee (MC) of the Chiefs of Defence Staff normally represented by military delegates to give military advice to the political and security committee. It started work in early 2000 with 10 to 15 officers under a colonel but will grow to 90. The permanent head is likely to be Javier Solana
- EU Military staff will support the Common European Security and Defence Policy (CESDP) including a situation centre

○ Principles for co-operation with non-EU European NATO members and other European partners in EU-led military crisis management have yet to be agreed
○ Member States will be required to improve national and multinational military capabilities, which will at the same time strengthen the capabilities of NATO. It is not yet clear how this will be done and what targets will be set
○ Joint national HQs will be opened to officers from other member states
○ A European air transport command will increase the numbers of readily deployable troops
○ Strategic airlift capacity is to be improved
○ Russia, Ukraine, and other European countries may be invited to take part in EU-led operations
○ Ways to be developed for full consultation, co-operation and transparency between the EU and NATO, taking into account the needs of all EU Member States
○ A non-military crisis management mechanism will be established to co-ordinate and make more effective the various civilian means and resources, in parallel with the military ones, at the disposal of the EU and Member States.
○ A Satellite Centre, an Institute for Security Studies and other resources

What European Leaders Said In 1999 About The EU Army

President Chirac said on Bastille Day, 'Europe will only really exist once it builds a credible defence capability.'

Chris Patten, the first EU Commissioner for External Relations, hoped for a Eurocorps 'operational in the not too distant future' but carefully avoided commenting on the idea of a European army and emphasised the umbrella of NATO. His job is to handle wider foreign policy issues including day-to-day diplomatic contacts.

Romano Prodi, the EU President, declared a unified European army would define his term in office that had just begun.

'The commission will use all the means at its disposal – single market legislation, competition and trade policy to develop a European defence industry.'

Handelsblatt 2.12.1999

Javier Solana, the EU's foreign and defence minister, told the European Parliament on 17th November 1999 that his key concerns were relations with Russia especially over the war in Chechnya, the reconstruction of Kosovo, Bosnia, the Middle East peace process, and Algeria. His list highlights the difference between a British foreign policy backing British global interest and a German-led EU foreign policy facing to the east.

Rudolf Sharping, Germany's Defence Minister, called for the EU to set up a joint air transport command in the first months of 2000 with a choice between the European Airbus A400M still on the drawing board and planned for 2006, and the Russo-Ukrainian Antonov 70. He studiously avoided the proven American C-17. In the interests of EU defence Britain has since agreed to the Airbus.

Sharping told the *Financial Times*,

> 'I hope it is in the interests of every European country . . . to drive forward European integration. To put it crudely, we have too much agricultural policy . . . and not nearly enough foreign policy.'

President Chirac in an anti-American speech in Paris to the IFRI conference on 4th November 1999 and widely reported in the American media, advocated a 'balanced' relationship of the world's major powers which could exist,

> 'only if the EU itself becomes a major pole of international equilibrium, endowing itself with all the instruments of a true power.'

Lord Robertson, the newly appointed Secretary General of NATO, said on the BBC news on 25th November 1999,

> 'Those in America who are becoming nervous about some of the developments that are taking place are wrong. Nothing being done in Europe at the present moment threatens the Alliance.'

Iain Duncan-Smith, the Opposition defence spokesman, opined on the same programme,

> 'This whole deal plays to a French agenda which has been going on for 40 years which is about dividing NATO.'

Dr. Javier Solana said in Berlin on 17th December that,

> '[The EU's defence and foreign policy] touches at the very heart of the nation state . . . as the union enlarges . . . we have . . . to take more responsibility for regional security, particularly in those areas bordering the Union *where we have direct interests at stake*. We also have to be prepared, where necessary, to use all legitimate means to project security and stability beyond out borders. And we need to be able to assert our values of humanitarian solidarity and respect for human rights . . .

> 'We will also be moving rapidly on response to the mandate given by Helsinki, to establish a co-ordinating mechanism for civilian crisis management.

'We need to continue to ensure that European defence industries restructure. We need greater co-operation and harmonisation of our planning requirement and our procurement policy.'

Solana sang the usual chorus, 'it is not about collective defence. NATO will remain the foundation of the collective defence of its members.'

Tony Blair repeated to the House of Commons on 13th December that,

'these arrangements, as the Helsinki council made clear explicitly, do not imply a European army . . . it reinforces NATO . . . '

William Hague replied,

'The decision to establish a defence identity outside NATO is momentous – it is one of the biggest changes in foreign and defence policies on which the government has embarked. We believe it has profound dangers.'

America Fears The End Of NATO

Throughout 1999 the Americans became increasingly alarmed by the EU threat to NATO. They were not fooled by the constant lip service that Europeans paid to NATO or by the EU's lack of battle readiness.

Henry Kissinger wrote on Kosovo in the *Washington Post* in August 1999,

'Those who sneer at history obviously do not recall that the legal doctrine of national sovereignty and the principle of non-interference – enshrined . . . in the UN Charter – emerged at the end of the devastating thirty years war, to inhibit a repetition of the depredations of the 17th century, during which perhaps 40 per cent of the population of Central Europe perished in the name of competing versions of universal truth . . . In the Clinton/Blair version of allied policy, NATO must act because it is the only posse in town and because its motives are pure . . .

'Various declarations or 'spins' since Kosovo have stated, or implied, that humanitarian military inter-vention is not contemplated against major powers (China, Russia, India), against allies, against allies of major powers or countries far distant from Europe. Then what is left? It would be an odd revolution that proclaimed new universal maxims but could find no concrete application except against a single Balkan thug.'

General Wesley Clark said at a Milan conference on defence in August 1999,

'Europeans are not prepared to meet external threats including strikes by inter-continental ballis-tic missiles.'

General Michael Short commented that European armies are hopelessly out of date,

'I can only hope that Western European countries will do everything they can to close this gap.'

The German General Klaus Naumann observed,

'The gap between the military capacities of American and NATO members is so great that it affects our combat co-operation.'

Alarmed at the disparity in arms, the US Defence secretary, William S. Cohen, told the September 1999 NATO ministers' conference,

> 'We envision the NATO countries acquiring . . . precision-guided munitions.'

Precision-guided munitions are not even on the EU's shopping list.

The division between Britain and the US was laid bare on 7th October 1999 when Lord Robertson, the new NATO secretary general, backed the EU line at Chatham House in London,

> 'We want to ensure that strong and effective military resources are also available to the EU, so that we can take action in support of the CFSP when NATO . . . is not engaged militarily.'

Speaking on the same platform Strobe Talbot, the American Deputy Secretary of State, immediately warned that EU defence role should stay within NATO and not be developed at the alliance's expense,

> '[The Cologne declaration] could be read to imply that Europe's default position would be to act *outside* the alliance wherever possible . . . The test of the European Security and Defence Identity should be will it work and will it keep NATO together . . . We would not want to see an ESDI that comes into being first *within* NATO but then grows *out of* NATO and finally grows *away from* NATO . . . that could eventually compete with NATO.'

The American Ambassador to NATO, Alexander Vershbow, warned in December 1999,

Europeans Abroad As Seen From America

John R. Bolton of the American Enterprise Institute in testimony to a Congressional Committee, November 1999

' . . . in pre-Maastricht days, decision making in the EC had very little real impact on the United States.

'Beginning approximately with the signing of the Maastricht Treaty (and in some cases before), this situation began to change dramatically, and has continued to evolve rapidly since . . . EC members came increasingly to unified positions before . . . bargaining began with non-EC members . . . this practice was initially hard for Americans to understand, and harder still to accept . . .

'[In] UN organisations, political consensus-building often occurs in discussions within the regional groupings, with the US belonging to the *Western European and Others Group*, or *WEOG*. In the late 1980's, EU members of this group unhesitatingly offered their individual national opinions on any topic under discussion . . .

'By 1992, however, the EU presidency always spoke alone, and . . . EU members themselves (or applicants), invariably deferred to the presidency. After the presidency announces the EU position, other EU members dutifully sit on their hands, while non-EU states debate in front of the silent, brooding EU. At times, the discussion reaches a point beyond the consensus previously established by intra-EU consultations, so the EU asks to suspend the WEOG meeting in order to caucus, and the EU members leave the room to await the next statement of the EU position. Thus, for many Americans, *European Political Co-operation* came increasingly to be understood as *American exclusion*.

'To be sure, these developments were not entirely uniform, and some rogue EU states, such as the United Kingdom, actually consulted much more closely with the United States throughout many diplomatic endeavors. But the overall pattern is unmistakable.'

'The Cologne decision seemed to suggest a desire on the part of the EU to become the 'option of first resort', rather than an alternative to NATO . . . the litmus test . . . is ultimately going to be whether the capabilities are there on the military side.'

Meanwhile isolationism was gaining ground in the US and Strobe Talbot warned,

'Many Americans are saying that never again should the US have to fly the lion's share of the risky missions in a NATO operation and foot by far the biggest bill . . . '

Scarcely reported in the British press, in November 1999 both Houses of Congress passed resolutions of concern about the European Security and Defence Identity, the Senate on 28th October 1999 and the House of Representatives on 2nd November 1999.

Representative Benjamin Gilman speaking on Resolution 59 said,

'To the degree that these initiatives are about European allies contributing more to our common defense within NATO, we applaud them. After all, most of us would have been delighted if our European allies had been able to handle the Bosnian crisis on their own or if they could have contributed more to the allied operations in Kosovo.

'But many of us are troubled by indications that these initiatives may be the first step toward a divorce between the European and North American pillars of NATO. Some of our European allies seem to long for an independent military capability, one that is not just separable from NATO, but that is separate.'

Despite the reservations of many in Washington about the general direction of EU defence the Clinton government was cautiously encouraging. Strobe Talbot was reported in the *Sunday Times* of 12th December 1999,

> 'We're not against it, we're not ambivalent, we're not anxious, we're for it . . . we want to see a Europe that can act effectively through the Alliance, or if NATO is not engaged on its own, through the EU. Period, end of debate.'

But Talbot noted two key phrases:

○ Of the St Malo agreement: 'national or multinational European means outside the NATO framework' and
○ Of the Cologne Summit declaration: the EU 'must have the capacity for autonomous action backed by credible military forces, the means to decide to use them and a readiness to do so'

Talbot argued,

> 'for those of us who have long supported the transatlantic security bond that is represented by NATO, these are troubling sentiments. If the European Union develops a security mechanism on the Continent that excludes not only our Nation but also all the other non-European Members of NATO, including such important allies as Norway, Poland, and Turkey, then very serious damage will have been done to the fabric of the transatlantic security bond, and the logic of the continued US security commitments to Europe that may be called into question.'

John R. Bolton of the American Enterprise Institute wrote in *The European Journal* of December 1999,

'If European countries wanted to strengthen their contribution to NATO they would increase their budgets in real terms and as a percentage of GDP. They are not doing so and total budgets are being squeezed because of EMU constraints. European checkbooks simply will not match the political rhetoric.'

Bolton noted that the EU 'neutrals of Austria, Finland, Sweden and Ireland were being drawn into the EU army.' He went on,

'An Austrian battalion is serving under German command in Kosovo but the Austrian constitution explicitly commits Austria to *permanent neutrality*, a condition imposed by the allies in 1955 precisely to stop the Austrian army from coming under the command of the German army ever again. Austria is now marching to a Franco-German tune. How long before the other neutrals do so too?'

Again Britain Reassures America But The Evidence Points Another Way

The British government tried to reassure the Americans that there was no hidden agenda to replace NATO and no plans to create a European standing army. On 26th January 2000 Britain's Defence Secretary, Geoff Hoon, told the Brookings Institute in Washington that 'Labour would never agree to plans that might jeopardise NATO' and 'we have no intention of moving towards a transnational army.'

Lord Robertson, the secretary general of NATO, did not give the Americans cause for complacency. He wrote in the *Financial Times* on 7th March 2000, 'a loose collection of states has become a union of unprecedented economic and political strength . . . it is only logical that [it] would want a credible role in defence.'

But he indicated that a complete break with the Americans and NATO would not happen,

'in the foreseeable future' but only because 'it cannot work. The US retains key strategic capabilities.'

Former Brigadier Geoffrey Van Orden MEP wrote in the *Wall Street Journal* on 25th November 1999,

'This will play into the hands of USA isolationists and leave the Western world divided at a time when there are real challenges and threats to be handled.'

Iain Duncan-Smith, the Shadow Defence Secretary said,

'This course will damage critically and even possibly destroy NATO. EU's plans for common defence are placing an artificial divide in the Alliance and will result in part of NATO's membership moving beyond the alliance.

'The UK's capability is beyond question but as it gets sucked in to this new defence posture that capability will begin to fall to a lower European common denominator.'

The EU may have set up a defence organisation but it rapidly became apparent that the money was not going to be available to sustain even the existing armed forces.

In January 2000 the German Finance Minister, Hans Eichel, cut £6.2 billion ($9.3 billion) from the German defence budget over the next four years. William Cohen, US Defence Secretary, said bluntly that it sent the wrong signal.

The EU may pretend that the new defence organisation is within NATO but the British split with its key ally the US is highly visible. On 8th October 1999 Blair, Chirac, and Schroder co-authored an op ed piece in the *New York Times* pleading with the US Senate not to reject the Comprehensive Test Ban Treaty. Ignoring them, the Senate overwhelmingly rejected the Treaty aware that the US needed to perfect national and theatre missile defence systems.

Bolton commented,

> 'If the best European argument is that NATO can only be preserved by the US leaving itself vulnerable to blackmail with weapons of mass destruction by rogue states, as Europe is, then NATO may be in terminal decline.'

An EU Intelligence Service Which Won't Be Secret

In December 1999 Schroder and Chirac for the Franco-German axis proposed an EU intelligence service and a network of spy satellites to back the Rapid Reaction Force. Britain objected to the spy satellites pointing out it would be cheaper to buy commercial photos. At present Britain has access to US satellite photography, which the EU is expensively planning to duplicate.

A Brussels funded think tank in London has even proposed that EU members including Britain should start sharing intelligence. They should set up their own Joint Intelligence committee (JIC) on the British model with the heads of US

A Republican View: Senator John McCain

'I feel it necessary to observe as we approach the 50th anniversary of NATO that the Atlantic Alliance is in pretty bad shape . . . The problem is threefold. First, our allies are spending far too little on their own defense to maintain the alliance as an effective military force. The day is fast approaching when each member's forces won't even be able to communicate with each other on the battlefield. Second, Europe's growing determination to develop a defense identity separate from NATO. Once only the product of French resentments, the idea of a separate defense identity is now even entertained in London. We must be emphatic with our allies. We encourage their efforts to assume more of the burden of their defense, but only within the institutions of NATO. Defense structures accountable to the WEU or any other organization other than the alliance will ultimately kill the alliance.

It is not hard to envision our allies intervening militarily, under the auspices of their new defense organization and without our concurrence, in very difficult problems that they are unprepared to resolve, necessitating an eventual appeal to NATO to bail them out. The American public's support for our membership in NATO would soon evaporate in these circumstances.

That support will also soon disappear if the United States and its NATO allies cannot come to an agreement on when they should act in mutual defense of each other's interests outside Europe. I supported the President's decision to deploy US forces to Bosnia. I will, with several important reservations support our involvement in Kosovo if we reach some agreement to do so. But I am in the minority on that issue. Most Americans cannot see the connection between our security and Mr. Milosevic's crimes.

They can, however, see the impact of Saddam's refusal to honor the terms of the Gulf War ceasefire, and they can't understand why most of our NATO allies refuse to help us enforce those terms. Most Americans recognize the threat of proliferation, and they can't understand why our allies dismiss our efforts to keep rogue states from acquiring these weapons.

I want NATO to endure for another fifty years or another century, for that matter. But if we must bear the greatest share of our mutual defense, then our allies must pay as much attention to our concerns, in and out of Europe, as we must to theirs. If not, the alliance might not last another decade. And that would be a genuine tragedy.'

From a Kansas State University lecture, 15.3.1999

intelligence agencies attending. In return the EU should be represented on Washington's National Security Council, wrote Charles Grant in *Intimate Relations* for the Centre for European Reform in May 2000.

On intelligence matter American and British interests have nearly always been close. The Americans have never been close to any other European country for security reasons, as one intelligence officer remarked 'most European countries leak like sieves.' Or as EU apologist Quentin Peel wrote in the *Financial Times* on 27th January 2000,

'One of the EU's great strengths is precisely that secrets are so hard to keep.'

The British Defence Industry May Be Hit Hard

In 1993 a declaration attached to the Maastricht Treaty gave the authority for a feasibility study for a European Armaments Agency (EAA). As a result in November 1996 the Western European Armaments Organisation (WEAO) was established with legal personality as a half way house to a European Armaments Agency.

Also in 1996 Britain, France, Germany, and Italy launched the Organisation for Joint Armament Co-operation (OCCAR) to manage defence procurement collaboration. That too has legal identity.

EU collaboration has already partly ended the arrangement that each country got a share of defence work in proportion to the equipment it bought. Since Britain is a major buyer it has also been a major recipient of defence orders. The House of Commons Defence Committee welcomed the new system in December 1999 because the MPs said it would increase competition. That seems optimistic given the extent of state intervention in European industry. It is more likely that the British defence industry would lose substantial orders.

European defence manufacturers are already consolidating in response to developing EU procurement and encouraged by Brussels. For example, in 2000 the European Aeronautic, Defence and Space Company (EADS) was created combining France's Aerospatiale Matra, and Germany's DASA. The EU believes that companies like this will be able to compete head to head against US companies, especially Boeing, Raytheon and Northrop-Grumman. It seems unlikely that a European consolidation of defence industries will really make a difference either to costs or to capability.

Sir Colin Chandler of Vickers plc wrote damningly in evidence to the Commons Defence Committee on 5th August 1999,

> 'We have never been sure of the purpose of OCCAR
> . . . what, exactly, it is that OCCAR is intended to
> do that hasn't been done before. It cannot hope to
> create a commercial environment which will condi-
> tion sovereign industries into more *European* com-
> binations – at least until . . . the contributing nations
> (except the UK) have either denationalised their
> own defence industries or stopped the national sub-
> ventions which keep many of them going. At the
> same time, it could not improve on the arrange-
> ments . . . to deliver collaborative projects – nor
> could it *save* a project if the political consensus for
> it began to break down. It could, though, deliver a
> large management overhead, loss of focus and
> breakdown in accountability.'

In December 1998 a group of experts started to meet every month to plan the European Armaments Agency with a 2001 deadline. The new agency will almost certainly take over from the national defence procurement agencies. The ramifications are enormous,

○ The British defence industry, the second largest in the world, may be badly hit as other EU countries take more of the orders. Almost certainly the EAA will be buying in Europe and not from the Americans or else-where.
○ EU procurement adds impetus to the drive for one civil law in the EU. Answering the question 'What happens if parties do not deliver' before the House of Commons Defence Committee, Sir Robert Walmsley, Chief of Defence Procurement replied 'we would very much like

to see harmonisation of commercial law in Europe and we would very much like a European Company statute. That would certainly help.'

The OCCAR Convention: Report and Proceedings of the Committee with Minutes of Evidence and Appendices
6.12.1999

○ The Blair government is spurning American equipment in favour of the EU. In May 2000 the British government committed to buying Meteor air-to-air missiles from an EU consortium; it gave a conditional undertaking to order the airbus A400M provided other countries do the same. The British Secretary of State for Defence told the Commons 'of our strong commitment to enhance European defence capabilities.'

○ EU requirements will be increasingly harmonised and geared to fighting Kosovan and Bosnian style wars on the eastern and south-eastern borders of the EU.

○ Defence research and development in the EU will be 'harmonised' and that may reduce the overall quality and spread a thin budget over a wider number of countries thus hitting British research.

Evidence to a House of Lords Select Committee highlighted this,

'An additional problem is the poor research and development practices in Europe. Evidence from Mr. Lahoud made clear that *we are spending, in Europe, less money on this activity and we are spending it in a less efficient way.* The US spends $35 billion per year on defence research and development (R&D) whilst the remainder of NATO spends only $9 billion. While the European members of NATO together spend about 60 per cent of the US figure on overall defence, duplication and inefficient national practices means they come nowhere near generating 60 per cent of the US capability. Unless this is addressed, the widening technology gap will soon lead to European troops being unable to operate alongside American troops because of their *technological backwardness.*'

Para 67, The Common European Policy
On Security And Defence

It Is An EU Army

'When I was talking about the European army, I was not joking...If you don't want to call it a European army, don't call it a European army...You can call it 'Margaret', you can call it 'Mary-Anne', you can find any name, but it is a joint effort for peace-keeping missions – the first time you have a joint, not bilateral, effort at European level.'

President Prodi to The Independent newspaper, 4.2.2000

Germany's Chancellor Schroder told the French National Assembly on 30th November 1999 that the key defence decisions would be taken under the French presidency in the second half of 2000, presumably when Germany could be sure of compliance with German wishes. In November 2000 the EU countries put their defence assets on the line at a capabilities commitment conference. The new force, bigger than expected, numbered 90,000 military personnel, 350 aircraft and 80 warships. The former long-term neutral countries of Austria and Ireland both did a *volte face* and committed troops.

To near total condemnation and outcry in Britain and the US the British government committed 24,000 troops, plus some additional army logistics units, 72 combat aircraft and 18 warships – half the Royal Navy. For servicemen, owing allegiance to the Queen and to Britain, fighting and perhaps dying for the EU, a new country, will present a challenge that could stretch the British forces to breaking point.

The new EU army commander or Director General is the German, Leit General Rainer Schuwirth, an officer without any combat experience.

There will be more bargaining to come over the as yet unmentioned French and British nuclear assets.

Longer term planning for an integrated EU army has started. A training and education strategy for all three British services will begin in 2010. What were once British training programmes will then take into account the new European army. The British government ordered a one-year review of all training including the Royal Naval College at Dartmouth, the Royal Military Academy at Sandhurst and the Royal Airforce College at Cranwell. It is being carried out by Vice-Admiral Jonathan Band to report in February 2001.

Other EU officers will attend courses to further closer integration and British officers will carry out part of their training in other EU countries. One MOD official told *The Times* on 24th February 2000 that 'we could have a European army by 2010' and therefore stronger links with staff colleges elsewhere in the EU would be necessary. More languages will be necessary for the polyglot army.

This mirrors what is *already* happening to the British police forces (see page 70).

The German army has planned to re-organise. On May 6th 2000 the former German President, Richard von Weizsacker, recommended,

○ Cutting the German army to 240,000 combat soldiers
○ Reducing the number of conscripts to just 30,000 from

130,000 so weakening the link between German society and the military which has been so carefully fostered for the last 45 years

○ Increasing the German Rapid Reaction Force from 50,000 to 140,000

○ Increasing the power of the inspector general, so forming a 'mini-General Staff' for central planning. The German General Staff was banned after both World Wars. The armed forces, reformed in the 1950s, were run by an inspector-general, which worked for an army limited to home defence and using NATO planning. The system no longer works now that German forces are routinely deployed abroad

With fewer conscripts and more professionals Germany will have greater freedom of action and a more efficient army than it has had at any time since its defeat in 1945. That should give pause for thought to some of its neighbours such as France and Poland. Longer term, Germany's ability to conduct Kosovo-level operations will be improved. Germany may even go it alone for some operations, for example a 'crisis' in Kaliningrad (formerly German Koenigsberg) or even the Baltic States.

Meanwhile President Prodi was right with his claim that there is an EU army, and NATO, the keeper of the peace in Europe for 50 years, now looks as though it is in terminal decline.

Today Europe is a much more unstable place. The over-riding questions are to what use will this new underfunded, undertrained and underarmed force be put; will it be capable of fulfilling the EU's ambitions, and if it fails who will pick up the pieces?

What is certain is that the EU army will not be defending Britain's interests. The Blair government has betrayed Britain and the British armed forces.

Chapter 7

POP GOES THE EURO

The Strength of Sterling

Most European countries . . . have repeatedly had to carry out changes, which have drastically altered their internal currencies . . . However, the pound as a unit of account has never had to be replaced by a 'new pound' or any other designation in 1,300 years, in contrast to the French franc or the various German currencies such as the Reichsmark, Rentenmark, Ostmark and Deutschmark, to mention merely some of the more modern changes.

Glyn Davies in 'A history of money from
ancient times to the present day'

For over 900 years, England has enjoyed a relatively stable single currency. The origins of sterling as England's single currency go back even further to 928, King Athelstan and the *Statute of Greatley*.

Today a British government is planning to abolish sterling and adopt a foreign currency. The single most important step to create one European country is to abolish the national currencies and introduce a European currency.

The risks of doing it are extremely high.

- There has never been a successful monetary union *before* a currency union
- Monetary unions either lead to political union or they fail

The Stages of EMU

Stage 1

1990 – The ERM: exchange controls between eight countries ended.

Stage 2

1994 – A Monetary Institute to oversee EMU in Frankfurt, with very tough convergence criteria set by the German Bundesbank for countries wishing to join. The Bundesbank hoped the criteria could not be met and the Deutschmark's independence could continue.

Stage 3

1999 – The European Central Bank began operations in Frankfurt. The euro was launched.

A new ERM for would-be EMU members was launched. Greece and Denmark are members: their currencies are pegged to the euro. Britain and Sweden are not members.

Stage 4

2002 – euro notes and coins to be issued and national currencies abolished.

○ There has never been a monetary union on the scale of the euro

○ If a country finds the going too tough there is no plan B, no rescue option

○ The EU countries' *political* commitment to the euro is so high that they are unlikely to allow it to fail at the first hurdle, or the second or even the third. Economies will be distorted to overcome euro crises. That could force a recession or worse

○ Britain is outside Euroland but the British taxpayer is already paying heavily for conversion to the euro without his agreement

○ By EU law Brussels already tells the British government how to run the British economy and the currency (Articles 98 and 99, Treaty of Rome)

○ The penalty for the British government's failure to run the economy in the interests of the EU may be unlimited fines in the European Court of Justice (Articles 226 to 229)

Since the early years of planning for one European country, a single currency has been an essential ingredient, just as it was for the Roman Empire. Abolishing the national currencies with their notes and coins used every day was always likely to meet some popular resistance. This critical step has therefore taken a long time. Indeed complete monetary union needs far reaching political union to succeed. The one is completely intertwined with the other.

The History

1957 to 1963 – When the Treaty of Rome was signed monetary union was a political impossibility. Jean Monnet played a waiting game: he hoped British entry in the early 1960s would give the green light for one currency. When de Gaulle vetoed British entry Monnet abandoned the Action Programme for EMU.

1969 – With British entry back on the agenda the French, Germans and British agreed to transform the Common Market into an economic and monetary union (EMU), and begin political union, deepening first in order to widen.

1970 – The Werner Report recommended three stages to a Single Currency by 1980. Stage one, the 'Snake', started in 1971, so-called because the currencies were narrowly tied to each other. It collapsed with the Bretton Woods currency system. Relaunched within a year Britain, Ireland, and Denmark joined. It collapsed again because of the oil shocks of 1973 and 1974.

1976 – Roy Jenkins launched the European Monetary System (EMS) as the big idea for his Presidency of the Commission. He deliberately went for a half way house: not yet a monetary union. Though the EMS was intentionally outside the Treaty of Rome, every country was committed to it.

At its heart was the Exchange Rate Mechanism (ERM) but again, playing safe, no timetable was set for countries to join. Each currency was allowed to fluctuate broadly around central rates with a top and bottom limit.

1979 – All the EEC countries, except Britain, joined the ERM.

1985 – EMU was included in the Single European Act, in the usual vague, preliminary co-operative terms.

1987 – Jacques Delors, the French President of the Commission, used the Stock Market Crash as the excuse to restart EMU. The Single Market, he said, needed a Single Currency to work.

Despite British government policy, Nigel Lawson, the

Chancellor of the Exchequer unofficially made sterling shadow the Deutschmark: the back door to the ERM. Interest rates were low to suit Germany so the British economy boomed and inflation shot up.

1989 – The Delors Committee declared, with no proof, that EMU would bring economic benefits. Currencies were to be fixed for all time in a three-stage process culminating in 1999. An orchestrated chorus of voices called for Britain to join the ERM and onward to a Single Currency.

1990 – Britain joined the ERM

16th September 1992 'Black Wednesday' – Britain was forced out of the ERM. Britain's bank rate rocketed to 15 per cent. The country fell into a deep recession. As a result:

o 1.75 million home owners were thrown into negative equity
o 100,000 businesses went bankrupt
o Unemployment doubled

Euro Creep To The East

Much of Eastern Europe and the Balkans, countries closely linked economically to Germany for a long time, are now nearly in Euroland because their currencies are pegged to the German mark.

In the Balkans, the Bosnian Mark is pegged to the German mark; Montenegro has introduced the German mark as a parallel currency alongside the Yugoslav dinar; Kosovo's official currency is the mark.

In Eastern Europe, Hungary dropped the US dollar from its currency basket in January 2000. The Hungarian forint is now exclusively based on the mark. The Bulgarian, Estonian and Lithuanian currencies have currency boards fixed to the German mark.

Euroland: Who Is In?

11 of Europe's 43 countries: France, Germany, Luxembourg, Belgium, Holland, Italy, Spain, Portugal, Finland, Austria, and Ireland are informally known as Euroland. Together they have a population of 290 million. Only two of the original 11 met the convergence criteria, Luxembourg, and Finland. Fudge on a gigantic scale was used to meet the Bundesbank's deliberately forbidding criteria.

Greece will abandon the drachma and adopt the euro on 1st January 2001. Greece had wanted to join from the beginning, but did not meet the Maastricht Treaty criteria then and does not now. It is yet another political decision made without economic backing.

Euroland: Who Is Out?

Denmark opted out of EMU, but has remained a member of the EMS, which linked its currency tightly to the euro. Danish voters said 'no' or 'nej' to joining the euro in a referendum on 28th September 2000 by 53.1 per cent against 46.9 per cent. Nearly 90 per cent of the electorate voted.

Denmark was the only country to have a referendum on the euro. No other nation has been allowed a democratic vote. In Denmark 47 of the 48 newspapers campaigned for the euro, as did the government all major political parties, the trade unions and big businesses. They did so with Danish and EU money.

Sweden and Britain voluntarily declined to meet the Maastricht criteria by refusing to join the EMS. They may yet have referendums to decide whether or not to abolish their currencies.

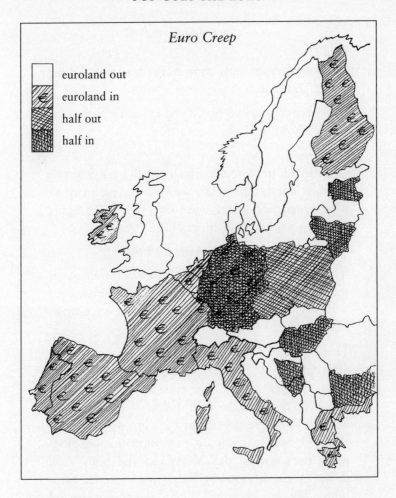

Euro Creep

euroland out
euroland in
half out
half in

The Czech Republic and Poland, which are among the five countries likely to join the EU next, will have to adopt the euro straight away. There can be no opt out for them. At present they both have currencies pegged to a basket of currencies including the US dollar.

Press Reaction

Day One

'The euro immediately contests the hegemony of the dollar.' *Le Monde*

'Parents and markets overjoyed at euro's birth – the dollar's hour of truth.' *Libération*

Day Two

'The British in their fine pinstripes did not want to get their hands dirty while we were toiling away on the construction of the euro. Our pound is staying out, they said, with stiff upper lip.' *Der Bild*

'London is isolated.' *Stuttgart Zeitung*

'Caught between the two huge blocs of the euro and the dollar' there will be 'a hasty and spontaneous British entry into the European monetary union.' *Handelsblatt*

Three Months Later

'The euro has made a bad start and there's no telling where this will end . . . the euro has lost credibility and will continue to fall. I fear a stampede as investor's rush to get out of the currency like lemmings. I can't exclude an explosion if unemployment rises, public deficits exceed the limits laid down by the Maastricht Treaty, and interest rates jump. We are entering a very dangerous period which could end with an orderly delay to the timetable for issuing (euro) coins and notes.'

Prof. Wilheim Noelling, Director of the Bundesbank 1982 to 1992, Hamburg, March 1999

One Year later

The euro no longer hit the headlines in the Continental press.

Press Reaction To The Euro Launch

The euro was launched on 4th January 1999 to a great fan-fare. The oddest sight was the Euroland finance ministers standing for a formal ovation to a British civil servant, Sir Nigel Wicks. For five years Sir Nigel chaired the EU Monetary Committee and led the technical preparations for the euro. They said they could not have done it without him.

In its first year, the euro fell in value by nearly 30 per cent against the US dollar and nearly 15 per cent against the pound sterling. Inflation is rising as imports especially oil become more and more expensive.

Percentage movement of Euro against US Dollar and £ Sterling

4 January 1999 to 31 October 2000

Source: BMDF / Market data prices

Money has been flooded out of the euro and shows no sign of abating. In May 2000 alone £10.6 billion left Euroland, that is at the rate of £127.2 billion a year or about £500 million every working day.

Economic Government Or Bust

To make one currency work there has to be one tax system, one social security system, in fact an economic government. All EU countries have to operate as one economy so countries on the fringes of the EU need big subsidies to survive. Just as Britain gives grants and subsidies to help poorer regions, so the same is true of the EU.

It would be very expensive for Britain. A 1977 EU report, *The MacDougall Report,* calculated that nearly ten per cent of the Community budget would be needed to offset the effects on the poorer regions. That may be optimistic: in the US funds needed to hold the country together could be as high as 20 per cent of the US budget. The British contribution alone would have to increase by a minimum of eight times and perhaps many times more than that.

It was therefore not surprising that no sooner had the euro been launched than the Bundesbank was calling for EU control over tax and public expenditure. The Bundesbank had direct experience of the bottomless pit of monetary union. In the ten years since the creation of the monetary union between West and East Germany, West Germany transferred over £500 billion ($750 billion) to the East and yet in March 2000 East Germany asked for another £100 billion ($150 billion).

When a few countries are forced to pay high taxes so others can enjoy a high standard of living the resentment could even cause the EU to break up.

One Size Cannot Fit All

'A European Currency will lead to member nations transferring their sovereignty over financial and wage policies as well as in monetary affairs. It is an illusion to think that states can hold onto their autonomy over taxation policies.'

Hans Tietmeyer, former President of the German Bundesbank,
quoted in Bill Jamieson's 'Britain a Global Future'

Joining EMU means handing over control of,

○ Interest rates
○ Exchange rates
○ All gold and foreign exchange reserves

National central banks have become branch banks of the European Central Bank. That is a fate that awaits the Bank of England if Britain joins the euro. Nearly all Central Bank Governors have readily embraced EMU. They were unable to resist the lure of 'independence' from their national governments, which was a precursor to full monetary union.

National governments within Euroland can never again be masters of their own economies. They can no longer control their own competitive position and, if hard times hit, they can do little to save jobs. Only two safety valves remain – cutting wages and cutting jobs.

Thirteen years ago France and Germany locked their currencies together. Today their unemployment rate is three times higher than in Britain. Official figures are certainly optimistic. Real unemployment may be around 20 per cent (officially 11 or 12 per cent).

Watch Ireland!

Ireland could be the first Euroland country to give up the euro. The Irish economy is similar to Britain and dissimilar to the rest of the EU. Anxious to do anything to distance itself from Britain, Ireland joined EMU and the euro at the first opportunity in January 1999. The results were immediately worrying, as the Irish press regularly reported.

A weak currency, low real interest rates and £1.3 billion ($20 billion) in tax cuts have all helped to fuel an economic boom and high inflation. House prices soared: the average cost of a house in the Irish Republic is now a third more than a British equivalent. Private credit is growing at 25 to 30 per cent a year compared with the average for Euroland of 10 to 11 per cent.

Inflation has rising sharply: from 1.2 per cent in July 1999 to 4.9 per cent in March 2000, and 6.2 per cent in July 2000. The British figure is 0.6 per cent. Even the *harmonised* EU measure of inflation (the HCIP) is 5.9 per cent, the highest in the EU.

Inflation is being imported. Businesses are threatened as essential imports from Britain cost more and more as the value of the euro collapses. Ireland depends heavily on Britain and the US for trade: Ireland is the fifth largest consumer of British goods in the world. The other Euroland nations do 90 per cent of their trading with each other so their economies are not threatened in the same way.

Travelling to Britain is now very expensive for the Irish.

Not only is the euro weak but the oil price, denominated in US dollars, is high. Rising energy costs mean rising prices for manufactured goods.

Irish trade union leaders are arguing for big wage increases to meet higher prices. They have done a 'U' turn from the days when they pushed for Ireland to join the euro. Now they are up in arms.

The Irish government is taking a sanguine stance because the sad truth is there is little it can do. So far, it has frozen alcohol prices.

Ireland cannot long remain competitive. 'I keep telling everyone it can't go on – I sound like Cassandra,' said

Maurice O'Connell, Ireland's Central Bank Governor. 'But there's nothing we can do.'

Pedro Solbes, the EU Commissioner for Economic Affairs, warned the Irish to slow growth using fiscal policy. 'That's not politically feasible,' replied Charlie McCreevy, Ireland's finance minister. *(From Business Watch, Channel 4 News, 22.6.2000)*

Irish Independent editorials routinely bemoan Ireland's fate,

> 'We are now hooked to a currency with little credibility in the foreign exchange markets. A weak euro may be useful for a fragile European economy in need of recovery but it is fuelling Ireland's economic boom to levels beyond our control. We cannot raise interest rates or revalue our currency to dampen demand. Ireland's government is marooned, behaving like a fire brigade without water trying to extinguish a blazing inferno.'
>
> *Irish Independent on Sunday, 30.4.2000*

> 'Clearly one interest rate does not fit all euro economies, no more than one drug would suit all patients with divergent medical conditions.'
>
> *16.7.2000*

Ireland does have options but all are unpalatable: taxes could go up, credit could be limited, price controls could be imposed or wages reduced.

If those fail, then the next stage will be bigger and bigger job losses and then waves of emigration. Ireland has experienced that tragedy before.

The Opt Out Is An Opt In

School Report

Name: **Britain**
Subject: **Economy**

The British government wrote in its compulsory 2000 annual report to the EU on British economic policy:

The updated programme presents the macroeconomic and budgetary perspectives for the period 1998-99 to 2004-05. Economic growth is expected to be around its trend rate over the period of the programme, estimated to be 2.5 per cent a year. The budget is expected to show small surpluses to 2001-02 and small deficits thereafter. The debt to GDP ratio is expected to fall to 38 per cent in 2004-05 . . .

The Commission marked it:

. . . It is therefore appropriate that the UK continues with the stability oriented policies which in turn, should help re-enforce a stable economic environment. ERM2 membership could add another pillar of stability to the effective fiscal and monetary framework already in place.

'Member states shall regard their economic policies as a matter of common concern and shall co-ordinate them within the Council . . . [to achieve] the objectives of the community . . .'

Articles 99.1 and 98 (title VII) of the Treaty of Rome

Both Britain and Denmark have an opt out from EMU in a protocol to the Maastricht Treaty. Despite those opt outs both countries are heavily constrained in the way they can run their economies. The Treaty of Rome says that the Commission can take Britain and Denmark to the European Court of Justice if their economies are not run on EU lines. The excuse could be anything from 'exporting unemployment', to 'unfair taxation', or 'competitive devaluation'. The penalty could be a heavy fine. The Commission provides the statistics to be used in Court: like any statistics they can be made to mean anything.

All Member States, whether in or out of the euro, have to avoid excessive government deficits: 3 per cent of the ratio of the planned or actual government deficit to GDP at market prices and 60 per cent for the ratio of government debt to GDP at market prices (Article 104.2 of the Treaty of Rome).

Britain agreed to the German designed Stability and Growth Pact in June 1997. It requires Britain and the other EU countries outside Euroland to report to Brussels every year on their convergence programmes. They have to say how they are meeting the objectives of the Pact. Britain has to be ready to join EMU, even if the British do not want to do so.

Peer group pressure helps the Stability Pact work. Any country that fails the test, faces large fines meted out by the European Court of Justice. Just the thought of being fined may goad finance ministers to toe the line. In practice, countries will probably be able to run excessive deficits for two years before incurring fines.

Although most British are against giving up the pound, the government is already making very expensive preparations to adopt the euro, paid for by every British tax payer.

Britain started to sell its gold reserves in July 1999. The price of gold fell steeply. The government intends to sell off 300 tonnes – more than half Britain's reserves – over a period of years. It says it will invest the proceeds in euros, yen, and dollars. The plan attracted widespread criticism, not least for its effect on the gold price and on gold miners in South Africa thrown out of work.

Britain Pays To Changeover Regardless

'I do not dismiss the constitutional or political issues, they are real. Monetary union is a big step of integration . . . There is much focus, which is entirely natural, on the politics of the euro project. It is of course an intensely political act.'

> Tony Blair, the British Prime Minister on the national
> changeover plan, Hansard, 23.2.1999

'We're being asked . . . to spend a £100 million fee for joining the euro, incur conversion costs estimated at in excess of £3 billion, inject £1 billion capital as our initial capital contribution, and introduce £500 billion of our currency reserves on a non-returnable basis – with no effective possibility of exit if it doesn't work out.'

> Jeffrey Titford, MEP and leader of UKIP,
> Chelmsford speech, 15.10.1999

The second national changeover plan, published in March 2000 by the Chancellor of the Exchequer, Gordon Brown, said that £6.3 million ($9.5 million) had already been spent to prepare for the euro since the first plan was published the year before. The timetable of two and a half to three years to replace the pound with the euro following a 'yes' vote was on track.

The plan now estimates it will take 2 billion euro notes and 13 to 14.5 billion coins to replace Britain's pounds and pence, a costly operation.

The government has ordered all government departments, including local government, to prepare for a fast transition to the euro after a referendum. By the end of 2000, direct departmental spending alone will be over £50 million ($75 million). The total central government cost may be as high as £3 billion ($4.5 billion), including the many government agencies.

The biggest of these is the National Health Service (NHS). Gigantic financial resources are being diverted from patient care. Managers of each health authority and trust have even been told to develop an 'education programme' for patients and their relatives about the euro's introduction (*from the NHS Finance Manual*).

The Finance Director of the Salisbury Health Care NHS Trust groaned that

'A huge amount of work is likely to be involved and substantial costs . . . there are no known benefits from this project, just a great deal of costs and hard work.'

Christopher Booker's column, Sunday Telegraph, 18.6.2000

The cost to convert British industry to the euro over three to four years may well be several billion pounds.

In Britain, outside the financial sector, euro use is low, at about one per cent of all transactions by British companies. Had the euro been essential for British business more companies would be using it by now.

It's Only Economics Says The Government

'The reason why people are against the Single Currency and us joining at the minute is probably the same reason I am, which is that the economics aren't right. If we suddenly had to join tomorrow we would have a very difficult economic situation because our economy is not in the same cycle as that of France and Germany at the moment.'

Tony Blair, the British Prime Minister,
on BBC Breakfast With Frost 16.1.2000

'Membership of the successful Single Currency, with a single market, which would be the largest single market in the world, a world into which we have over 50 percent of our trade and with which millions of British jobs are engaged, is in principle the right thing for Britain to do . . . Let's get one thing straight. If I recommend to the British people that we join the euro I will make the case for it as strongly and as powerfully as you could possibly hear.'

Tony Blair at a press conference at
the EU Summit in Portugal, June 2000

The British government has set only 'economic tests' to judge whether to join EMU and the euro. Those tests can be fudged just as the EU's convergence tests for Euroland membership were fudged.

The government has failed to mention political union and the end of independence, which must follow if monetary union is to be successful.

The Convergence Criteria
Labour's Five Economic Tests

Any Government decision to join the Single Currency at a future date will be based on what is in the national economic interest.

The Government will examine the following questions:

---

1 Would joining EMU create better conditions for firms making long-term decisions to invest in the United Kingdom?

2 How would being part of the Single Currency affect financial services?

3 Are business cycles compatible so that the UK and others in Europe could live comfortably with euro interest rates on a permanent basis?

4 If problems do emerge, is there sufficient flexibility to deal with them?

5 Will joining EMU help to promote higher growth, stability and a lasting increase in jobs?

From the Foreign Office web site www.fco.gov.uk

Ships That Pass In The Night: Britain Is Different

- The British economy is much more sensitive to changes in short term interest rates than the rest of the EU because of a much higher use of credit e.g. mortgages and credit cards
- Britain trades globally especially with the US and other dollar linked countries
- The 11 Euroland countries are largely economic satellites of Germany and France, unlike Britain
- More than four fifths of the British economy is *not* involved in trading with the EU
- The proportion of British exports to the EU – about 43 per cent – has been falling for the last decade
- Most British investment overseas goes outside the EU (over 80 per cent) and most investment into Britain comes from outside the EU (over 80 per cent)

○ Sterling is relatively stable against the US dollar

Can the British economy converge with the Continental economies *and* stay in line with them?

To do so the British government would have to,

○ Destroy large tracts of British business including North Sea oil and gas, aerospace and defence industries, pharmaceuticals, information technology, the City of London, because they are all largely denominated in dollars
○ End the British habit of home ownership in favour of the more usual continental practice of renting
○ Raise taxes dramatically
○ Increase welfare spending dramatically
○ Slash the funding of private pensions
○ Intensify business regulation
○ Massively reduce trade with the rest of the world and switch those exports to the EU

Britain would then effectively be an economic satellite of Germany and France, just like the other Euroland economies.

Europe's Economic Government

In 1999, the French led Euroland's eleven countries to set up Euro-X, a committee of Finance Ministers to watch over the Single Currency. Britain, as a non-euro country, is barred from even observing its meetings. The new 'Government' meets every month and Commission institutions report to it. Greece has now joined.

In June 2000 France and Germany decided to use this new 'Government' to create an inner core of countries ready to press ahead to closer union in economic affairs, as well as defence, foreign policy, and justice. They have agreed that majority voting should become the rule leaving the national veto only for constitutional issues, and matters of defence and national security. Thus, they intend to create pressure on those outside, like Britain, to join in.

Already Britain's economic position has been further weakened in international negotiations, notably in the G7. John R. Bolton of the American Enterprise Institute explained in testimony to a Congressional Committee in November 1999,

> 'In G7 consultations, the four European governments (France, Germany, Italy, the UK) increasingly co-ordinate their positions beforehand, leaving, Canada, Japan and the United States to be confronted with a united front by the European members of the group . . . the G7 now functions as a G4, with an EU representative literally and figuratively sitting in the vacant places of the Europeans.'

Equal to the US?

The Governor of the European Central Bank now represents the Euroland countries on the G7. France and Germany are no longer part of the G7 as of right.

If Britain adopts the euro it too will lose its seat at the G7 table. The G7 will then become the G3 of the US, Japan and the EU.

According to Brussels the world will then be divided into three blocs and the EU will be at least as important as the US. Although the EU Commission would never admit it the reality is rather different. 80 per cent of the world's financial transactions and nearly 60 per cent of the world's commercial transactions are denominated in US dollars. 70 per cent of the

Continental EU's business transactions are in US dollars. There is no sign that is going to change.

The Inscrutable Central Bank

'The most independent central bank there has ever been' was how Martin Wolf of the *Financial Times* described the Bank to a House of Lords Select Committee. He contrasted it with the Bundesbank and the US Federal Reserve, which operate under arrangements that can be changed by a legislature. The ECB operates under a Treaty he described as 'effectively unamendable.'

'The European Central Bank: Will It Work?' House of Lords, 24th Report on the European Communities

9.6.1998

Unlike the Bank of England, the European Central Bank is extremely powerful.

- The Bank is accountable only to the toothless European Parliament
- The board of six bankers is in office for eight years
- They can only be sacked by the European Court of Justice
- The standards they have to maintain, and by which they can be sacked, are stated nowhere
- The Bank has 'to maintain price stability' but no figures are given
- The Bank is forbidden by treaty to publish the minutes of its governing council. It is claimed publication would encourage undesirable scrutiny of member's voting patterns and encourage pressure on the board from 'local', that is national, interests. Council members can hide

behind a cloak of confidentiality and no-one will know if
they *do* yield to political pressure
o The Bank has to issue just one annual report
o It is illegal for *democratically* elected politicians to seek
to influence the Bank

The German Bundesbank said that 'anything more than
consensus reports would cause confusion.' So far,

o The Bank has refused to publish two-year inflation fore-
casts, the cornerstone of monetary policy. The Bank
claims any forecast would be 'self-fulfilling'
o The Bank has set its own objective: price stability with an
inflation ceiling of no more than 2 per cent. There is no
floor, implying acceptance of deflation
o It says it will use a basket of other economic indicators.
But what indicators? They will not be published

Such a secret bank, run by unaccountable bankers, in
office for long periods, cannot command any public support. Paul Volcker, a former chairman of the US Federal
Reserve Board, told the Lords Select Committee that a central
bank,

'would not survive or conduct appropriate policies
over a long period unless it could command public
support . . .'

'Doomed to Failure'

In March 1998 the Bundesbank directors reported to the
German Federal Cabinet that the euro was doomed to failure.
Their report said that the euro project, on technical grounds
alone, was a hazardous and reckless venture and not least

Can The European Central Bank Survive?

'From now on, monetary policy, usually an essential part of national sovereignty, will be decided by a truly European institution.'

Wim Duisenburg, The Daily Telegraph, 1.1.1999

'The credibility of the ECB will depend on its transparency and willingness to establish a dialogue with the European public. It must establish a regular reporting system.'

Gordon Brown, Chancellor of the Exchequer,
the Financial Times 8.4.1998

'It is counterproductive to publish minutes too soon, minutes should be published after 16 years.'

Wim Duisenberg, the Dutch President of the European Central
Bank, replying to the European Parliament, May 1998

'The envisaged combination of plentiful discretion with negligible transparency is more than unacceptable. It is highly dangerous.'

A Financial Times report, 15.10.1998

'Germans had been told the currency would be as strong as the market but have been very disappointed . . . People are losing faith in the currency before they have even handled it.'

Jurgen Donges, the German economist chairing a committee
advising the German government on the euro to
The Daily Telegraph, spring 2000

because the necessary conditions supposedly required to ensure its success do not exist. *(Bundesbank Monthly Report, April 1998)*

Professor Norbert Berthold of the University of Würzburg wrote in *Handelsblatt* on 12.1.2000 that,

> 'the euro has good prospects only if certain conditions are fulfilled, principally that the countries forming the union are economically similar. In the euro-zone the structures of production are very different. Labour markets are too rigid. Therefore, wage levels cannot react sufficiently to regional or sectoral needs in the euro zone.
>
> 'For this to happen union power would have to be drastically reduced and the European social states would have to be largely privatised. All fiscal centralisation would have to be abandoned.
>
> 'In short, competition is necessary everywhere. That was true before the introduction of the euro. It is even truer now.'

Professor Berthold speculated that some countries might decide they are better off out of the euro than in. 'The costs of leaving are relatively small, at least until national currencies are physically abolished in 2002. It is therefore conceivable that some member states will leave the monetary union and stand on their own two feet again.'

Four leading German economists jointly warned that the euro may fall apart and plunge Europe into a financial catastrophe. They said in an article published in *The London Metro* on 6.6.2000 that European politicians trying to talk up the euro would not help. The EU's economic recovery and jobs market improvements were temporary because they were caused by the weak euro. The currency will face

To Political Union

'One must never forget that monetary union, which the two of us were the first to propose more than a decade ago, is ultimately a political project . . . Monetary union is a federative project that needs to be accompanied and followed by other steps.'

Giscard d'Estaing and Helmut Schmidt, former French and German leaders, International Herald Tribune, 14.10.1997

'Political and economic monetary union are inseparably linked. The one is the unconditional complement of the other.'

Chancellor Kohl in a speech in France, 3.12.1991

'We can preserve all our economic achievements only if we secure them politically. An economic union can only survive if it is based on a political union.'

Chancellor Kohl, the Financial Times, 4.1.1993

'It is now up to us to see that we embark on the next stage leading to political unity . . . the consequence of economic unity, so that Europe can in the future also play a political role on the international stage, leading even as far as a common defence policy.'

Jacques Santer, President of the European Commission, The Daily Telegraph, 1.1.1999

'The introduction of the common currency was in no way just an economic decision. Monetary Union is demanding that we Europeans press ahead resolutely with political integration.'

Gerhard Schroder, German Chancellor at ceremony on the retirement of Hans Tietmeyer, president of the Bundesbank, 30.8.1999 even greater problems when poorer countries from Eastern Europe become members of the monetary union. The old members will have to carry the burden of the weaker newcomers.

Even the ECB's chief economist, Professor Otmar Issing, had doubts. He wrote,

'The risk of failure can be summed up in a few words. An EU which enchains its huge innovative potential through all sorts of regulations, suppresses economic incentives through high taxes, seeks to protect its prosperity from the outside behind all sorts of barriers and strives to redistribute wealth internally, based on an ideology of equality portrayed as justice, renounces not only an important role on the world stage, but also its own future . . . Ideologies which are hostile to freedom and the market economy have proved extremely resistant in Europe.'

Article 'Europe: Common Money – Political Union' in
Economic Affairs: The Journal of the Institute of Economic
Affairs, March 2000

Americans Warn Of War

Milton Friedman told an interviewer

'Currency is a very important symbol of sovereignty. And it seems to me a nation, if it's going to stay a nation, needs as many symbols of sovereignty as it can possibly have.'

Forbes Magazine, 3.5.1999

Henry Kissinger, the former US Secretary of State, said in the *The Daily Telegraph* (7.5.1998) that Britain should not rush to join the Single Currency but ensure that the EU develops an open trading and strategic relationship with America. An inward-looking Europe, he said, built on the French model, as opposed to the more outward Atlanticist version favoured by the British, 'would imperil trans-Atlantic relations and create a dangerous power vacuum.'

Kissinger warned that the economic stresses of a more integrated Europe would,

> 'drive the EMU toward political union or toward disintegration . . . Should monetary union disintegrate, the Europe resulting from the collapse will be either extremely Left or extremely Right wing, or a combination of the two.'

In April 1998 Newt Gingrich, a former Speaker of the House of Representatives, described monetary union as 'an extraordinary gamble', which posed 'staggering' problems that Europe's immature political institutions might not be able to solve.

Martin Feldstein, Professor of Economics at Harvard University wrote in *Foreign Affairs*, Nov/Dec 1999,

> 'The Nazis used the same propaganda . . . The *thousand-year Reich* lasted twelve years. So much for inevitability . . . the shift to EMU and political integration that would follow it would be more likely to lead to increased conflicts within Europe and between Europe and the United States.

> 'A European Single Currency could cause wars between member states and provoke disputes between Europe and the United States. Rather than promoting international prosperity and harmony, monetary union would cause dangerous disputes over interest rate and employment policies.

'The European Central Bank would have to make monetary policy with a view to the conditions in all of Europe, not just a particular country or region. The result would be conflict between any country with rising unemployment and the rest of the EU . . . '

Professor Feldstein argued that EMU would lead to political union and the creation of a European foreign policy and military structure. This would pose potential conflicts of interest with the United States as well as tensions within Europe.

'Although it is impossible to know for certain whether these conflicts would lead to war, it is too real a possibility to ignore in weighing the potential effects of EMU and the European political integration that would follow.'

The US Federal Reserve Board has been diplomatically mute on the outlook for the euro. Governor Laurence H. Meyer did suggest that the euro could prove to be successful as a pricing mechanism but not as a monetary mechanism,

'A growing and ultimately significant international role for the euro is not automatic. Instead, the euro area will have to earn its place in the international financial system, and earn it the old fashioned way – by pursuing policies that produce a healthy euro-area economy. By improving price discovery within the euro zone, the euro itself may increase competitiveness across Europe, and thereby benefit low-cost producers, trade competitiveness, and European consumers.

'But the key to the success of the euro area would still appear to be the same set of policies that would have been essential in France, Germany, and other euro countries in the absence of the euro: structural reforms, especially those related to reducing the rigidities in European labor markets, and disciplined monetary and fiscal policies.

'Does the euro make structural reforms and disciplined policy more or less likely? Frankly, I do not know the answer to that question.'

Remarks by Governor Laurence H. Meyer at the European Institute's Conference 'Challenges to the European Millennium', 26.4.1999

The British Under Pressure

Opinion polls in Britain have regularly reported that over 70 per cent of British people want to keep the pound. Even the EU's *Eurobarometer* polls say the same.

Faced with the British people's hostility to giving up the pound the EU has backtracked.

In January 2000 Wim Duisenberg, President of the European Central Bank, told the BBC it could be years before Britain was ready to join the European single currency. Interviewed for the *Money Programme* he said 'We're talking about a moment in time which is years from today.'

The next day, perhaps not so coincidentally, the Confederation of British Industry stopped its pro euro campaign. Digby Jones, the new CBI chief executive, told the BBC that scrapping the pound and adopting the euro had been 'distracting' members from the issue of making the single market work.

Meanwhile the City of London has made money from the euro. For example, despite dire EU predictions, the City has increased its share of European capital market transactions. The Bank of England reported London's share of euro-denominated bond markets grew from 48 per cent to 58 per cent between the first and third quarters of 1999 alone.

On 14th June 2000, Sir Eddie George, the Governor of the Bank of England, said,

'There were those who argued that the City would suffer if the UK failed to join from the outset. That clearly has not so far happened – quite the reverse.'

Despite being confounded by events, doom mongers still argued that the City would suffer if Britain did not adopt the euro soon. London remained highly competitive. The Governor added the implication of such statements was 'that somehow or other obstacles will be put in our way.'

On 19th February 2000 Keith Vaz, the British Minister for Europe, claimed when interviewed by *The Daily Telegraph*,

'Out of Europe is out of a job. People don't understand that enough. If we pull out, our economy is going to be devastated and the European economy is going to be devastated and we can't afford that to happen. There are 3.5 million jobs directly linked to our being in Europe and that can only increase.'

Mr. Vaz felt so strongly about his claim that he toured Britain in a 'Eurobus' called Eunice accompanied by no less than five British diplomats. These civil servants were being wrongly used for party political promotion, to persuade the British of the case for the euro. On the tour between 29th November and 3rd December 1999 they visited universities and schools where Mr. Vaz took morning assembly. The British diplomats wore 'Your Britain, Your Europe' stickers. They handed out balloons, stickers, carrier bags and fact sheets highlighting the generous subsidies received from Brussels.

The Labour government has used the propaganda group, Britain in Europe (BiE), to back its claims that jobs would be lost on a huge scale if Britain kept the pound. It engaged Martin Weale, the director of the National Institute of

Economic and Social Research, to report on the impact of Britain staying out. Weale said pro-euro supporters had misused his report to make 'plain silly' claims about the impact of British withdrawal. So he deliberately boycotted the launch of the BiE poster campaign based on his research.

In July 2000, Brussels even agreed a plan to use school-children to sell the benefits of the ailing euro to their doubting parents. Children will be taught through essays, painting, and public speaking competitions. After the business community and children, the Brussels' propaganda programme will target women and minority groups. And the money is there to do it,

> 'The EU's true propaganda budget to prepare for
> the euro is estimated to be £2.7 billion each year.'
> *Hervé Fabre-Aubrespy MEP, speech to*
> *the EU Cardiff Conference, 14.6.1998*

While that EU propaganda budget has been scaled down after the euro launch what remains is sharply focussed on the four countries still outside Euroland. A huge range of tricks is being used to convince Britons they would be better off with the euro than the pound.

Here are some of them culled from the British press:

- 'Surveys' showing how expensive cars are in Britain compared with Euroland, forgetting to mention that the euro has devalued sharply against sterling
- Deliberately leaked reports from a British diplomat that Japanese manufacturers need Britain in the euro otherwise jobs will be lost
- Falsified trade statistics to show that Britain does most business with Euroland
- In April 2000 BMW of Germany blamed the pound's strength against the euro for the bulk of its losses at its

Rover car business. Its surprise sale of Rover in May
2000 jeopardised thousands of British jobs

○ In June 2000, Nissan UK threatened the loss of 12,000
jobs if Britain stayed outside the euro. Nissan UK is 37
per cent owned by the French company Renault and the
French government has a large stake

What A Risky Euro, Say The British

' . . . if the EU has to be sold to the British public, the
economic arguments have to be very delicately balanced.
It is necessary to be economical with the truth.'

Sir Peter Marshall, KCMG, address at
Royal Commonwealth Society, 23.3.1998

'It is a myth that entry will bring cheaper mortgages . . .
there is nothing to say that joining EMU [the euro] will
push mortgages down to European levels – we could see
them rise slightly in the short term.'

Mike Lazenby, Director of the Nationwide Building Society,
in The Sun, 28.5.1998

'I don't believe we are talking about the whole thing blow-
ing up, but my view is it will cause quite serious tensions.'

Sir Eddie George, Bank of England Governor, The Sun, 3.4.1998

'The euro is being sold to the British people rather successfully at present, by bogus argument that used to
belong to the Marxists, that of historical inevitability . . .'

William Rees-Mogg, The Times, 29.4.1998

'I think [the European public have] been given false
assurances that EMU itself will directly create jobs and
cure unemployment – an assertion without intellectual
justification.'

Adair Turner, CBI Director General, quoted in Freedom Today,
Aug/Sept 1998

'By that time [2002] a new entrant will be required to accept not just a Single Currency but a degree of harmonisation of fiscal and economic policy toward political union that the British electorate might not stomach.'

Roy Denman, former EU Commission representative in Washington, International Herald Tribune, 14.10.1998

'The referendum is likely to be called only if we show that we can win it. That is why we have been creating a campaign coalition to cover the whole country.'

The European Movement, 10.2.1999

' . . . monetary union is fundamentally a political rather than an economic issue.'

Sir Eddie George in a Speech 'Britain and Europe' to The British Swiss Chamber of Commerce on 12.9.2000

The Ultimate Threat

In March 2000, the EU Commission warned that Britain's longer-term membership of the EU could be called into question if Britain remained outside the Single Currency. Pedro Solbes, the commissioner in charge of EMU, told Danish journalists in Strasbourg that EMU was more than a mere currency arrangement and should be understood as a bridge to full political union,

'Part-time membership of the EU is not good enough. In the longer term it's not possible to be in the Union and outside EMU.'

The Daily Telegraph, 16.3.2000

Chapter 8

THE TAX MAN COMETH

Where The EU Gets Its Money

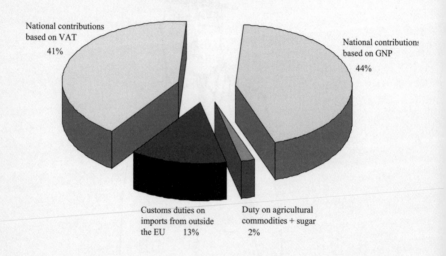

National contributions
based on VAT
41%

National contributions
based on GNP
44%

Customs duties on
imports from outside
the EU   13%

Duty on agricultural
commodities + sugar
2%

If you create a tax heaven for a few people, you condemn the rest to a tax hell.

Commissioner Mario Monte speaking to the City of
London on withholding tax, 12.5.1999

British Government Defends Loss of Tax Independence

In 1997 Lord Mackay, then Minister for Social Security, told
the House of Lords,

> 'My Lords, legislation on VAT and excise is estab-
> lished under Article 93 of the treaty. Customs duties
> are set under Articles 26 and 133 of the treaty.
> Direct taxation is primarily a matter for the
> Member States at national level and therefore
> the treaty's state aid rules and non-discrimination
> provisions are the only limitations on Member
> States in this field. Unanimity is required for all
> VAT, excise and direct tax legislation and
> Parliament has the opportunity to scrutinise all pro-
> posals. The Government will continue to defend
> that position.'

From a House of Lords Debate, 3.3.1997
(Treaty article numbers updated)

What Lord Mackay defended is a real loss of national tax
independence. Disguised simply as the numbers of treaty arti-

cles it may not readily appear to be so, and as this chapter will show, EU state aid rules severely limit tax independence.

Here are the three treaty articles the British government is defending,

> 'The Council shall, acting unanimously on a proposal from the Commission . . . adopt provisions for the harmonisation of legislation concerning turnover taxes [VAT], excise duties and other forms of indirect taxation . . . ' *Article 93*
> **The national veto still remains.**

> 'Common Customs tariff duties shall be fixed by the Council acting by qualified majority on a proposal from the Commission.' *Article 26*
> **There is no national veto.**

> 'The common commercial policy shall be based on uniform principles, particularly in regard to changes in tariff rates, the conclusion of tariff and trade agreements . . . the Council shall act by a qualified majority . . . ' *Article 133*
> **There is no national veto.**

A Call To Arms?

Countries do not readily agree to give up their right to raise money. No money means no government and effectively no country. The EU's attempt to build one tax system run from Brussels has already taken four decades. Today tax policy has reached the top of the EU agenda.

Already the EU effectively controls two major taxes, VAT and customs duties. Brussels has also had some success in extending its writ to business taxes, income tax and social security.

The way the EU does that is to extend the Single Market rules and that means no national veto. What the Commission says goes.

If Brussels does succeed in controlling *all* taxes, British taxes will go up by a minimum of one sixth to the present EU tax average. With an ageing EU population and a big EU budget the British could pay over a quarter more in taxes.

The EU needs more money. It has plans far exceeding its budget and its resources were capped in 1988 at 1.27 per cent of EU GDP. Now the euro has created an urgent need for huge regional grants for the poorer parts of Euroland. Without those grants there could be unrest, even violence.

Worst of all is the tax dictatorship. The elected representatives of the British people have no effective control over EU tax proposals. In 1776, the United States of America set a precedent on that very issue and declared independence from Britain. No taxation without representation was a powerful cry.

The lesson that taxation can provoke rebellion, even armed rebellion, has not been lost on Brussels. So, it is trying to make its true purpose as shadowy as possible. The Commission is now campaigning to end the chief obstacle it faces, the national veto on all tax and social security measures 'to ensure the proper functioning of the Single Market.'

How The EU Mounts Its Tax Attack

o Secrecy is a key weapon

'We are left in as much ignorance as anyone else about the way in which the Code of Conduct Group is going about its business. We think that the lack of transparency in the handling of this matter shows both the Council of Ministers and the Government in a very poor light. It leaves the Code of Conduct open to being described as an obnoxious method of inflicting secret taxation . . . '

House of Lords 15th Report on the European Communities, 'Taxes in the EU: Can co-ordination and competition co-exist?' 20. 7.1999

○ The European Court of Justice creates *British* tax law

'Effectively, the European Court of Justice has become a UK tax court.'

David Southern, a tax barrister, Taxation, 16.10.1997

The take-over of national tax law is largely happening quietly in the European Court of Justice in Luxembourg where Britain has no authority. The key tax articles in the Treaty of Rome are justicible by the Court. There is no scrutiny by elected British MPs; no banner headlines in the press; and as yet no public outrage at taxation without representation.

British VAT Tribunals and the High Court refer case after case to the ECJ to rule on tax issues the tribunal chairmen or judges deem contentious. It strikes down national tax laws if judges are incompatible with the Treaty of Rome.

The EU court rules, and returns the case for a *local* decision to be announced to the parties. A further precedent is set and written into *British* law. It is instant tax *harmonisation*.

National laws have been changed just by the threat of a referral to the ECJ. For example, Gordon Brown, the British Chancellor of the Exchequer, abolished Advanced Corporation Tax in his July 1997 budget because a similar case involving a German chemical company, Hoechst, had already been referred to the ECJ.

○ The Commission blackmails

However often the Government repeats that the Code is not legally binding . . . agreeing to it has obviously created a moral if not a legal obligation on the Government to 'roll back' tax measures which are ultimately deemed to be 'harmful', and not to introduce new measures of the same kind.'

House of Lords 15th Report on the European Communities, 'Taxes in the EU: Can co-ordination and competition co-exist?' 20. 7.1999

○ The Commission hoodwinks

The Commission tries to disguise its ends. It sets a *minimum* VAT rate of 5 per cent, or it *co-ordinates*, or it *harmonises*. It avoids spelling out what it is doing – creating one EU tax system.

VAT – *The First EU Tax*

1967 – The EEC started its own sales tax, value-added tax (VAT) part of which goes to Brussels (First VAT Directive). Even before joining the Common Market Britain replaced its purchase tax by VAT as a sign of its good intentions towards the EEC and at the same time as it introduced decimalisation and metrication.

1973 – By agreeing to the Treaty of Rome Britain gave up control of indirect taxation, a point which many British politicians have not still understood.

1977 – The EEC set a minimum VAT rate of 5 per cent via a labyrinthine law, the 6th VAT Directive. Member States agreed to 'adopt further directives . . . in order to achieve complete parallelism of the national tax systems.' And they did so by amending the 6th VAT directive 16 times and issuing another 90 or more directives.

1992 – The EU raised the minimum VAT rate to 15 per

Harmonise VAT!

'We arrived at the village of Rust on the edge of the Black Forest in Germany. The mayoral reception turned out to be a grand dinner. About one thousand guests were present. The hall was draped in blue, with large EU flags everywhere. The tablecloths were EU flags, the carpet was covered in EU flags and at the door we were given EU flag umbrellas. As we sat down a show began on the stage, which was flanked by two huge screens showing the performance. The entertainment and atmosphere was a cross between the Labour Party rally during the 1992 General Election and the opening night of the Millennium Dome. There were acrobats, dancers, jugglers, and all the while louder and louder music.

Then came the speeches. The opening address was given by the chief executive of the theme park that was paying host – no surprise to know that it was called *Europa Park*. In his third sentence he called for VAT harmonisation across Europe, which was met with rapturous applause.'

Nigel Farage MEP, UK Independence News, 17.5.2000

cent with a few goods and services still allowed either a 9 per cent rate or less or even zero rating. No upper limit has yet been agreed but the Commission has proposed 25 per cent. VAT rates and the goods to which they apply still vary greatly from country to country.

The VAT Overlord

For over 20 years a committee has worked in secret to chart the way to 'harmonise' VAT. In the EU Advisory VAT Committee there is no voting, no minutes are published and a consensus view 'emerges'. The Commission chairs it. The 6th VAT Directive set it up in 1977.

In 1997, the Commission proposed to turn the Advisory VAT Committee into a Regulatory Committee legislating for the whole EU. It would work by qualified majority voting, and end the national veto. The Member States have yet to agree to give up their remaining powers over VAT.

The Future Of VAT

In 1996 the Commission proposed a radical VAT system, still to be agreed. If the Commission prevails everyone will be able to see that VAT is an EU tax administered by Brussels. It could not then be mistaken as a national tax. The Member States will act as Brussels tax collectors and send *our* money to Brussels. The proposals include,

- A standard VAT rate of 18 per cent
- An unspecified reduced rate, presumably higher than the present 5 per cent (see box)
- The zero rate on food and other goods will be abolished (see box)

○ One place of registration for every business in the EU
○ A central EU tax collection and enforcement authority. For two years Customs and Excise has been co-operating on an EU wide system of VAT inspection. Some EU tax inspectors already exist under the Mergers Directive
○ A clearing house system to allocate money to 'needy' parts of the EU

Tomorrow these items could be taxed at 18 per cent,

> New houses and land, postage stamps, old buildings, land not for housing, passenger transport, electricity, natural gas, antiques, children's clothes, children's footwear, take-away meals, housing, food, books, newspapers, periodicals.

VAT Examples

○ **Taxing the net**
The Commission will almost certainly impose VAT on music, software, and other 'virtual' goods, like paid-for television, bought over the Internet when it can devise a system to do it.
○ **Taxing stamps**
By stealth the British government appears to have agreed VAT on stamps, a controversial issue. In 1999 the Royal Mail put up the cost of letters to other EU countries by 4p to 30p. That 4p is about the same as the proposed VAT. The increase will allow the government to agree to VAT, while telling the British public that there will be no increase in the price of stamps.
○ **Taxing roads and bridges**
The EU will be charging VAT on road tolls, bridges and tunnels at the full rate of 17.5 per cent backdated to

1994 because of a recent case in the European Court of Justice. The British government put up another robust defence and has now decided to absorb the tax rather than charge motorists directly.

Taxing Art

London has the second largest art market in the world (annual turnover £2.5 billion or $4 million) and is dominant in Europe. But that has only been the case for 50 years. Paris used to be the leading art market in Europe, until the French imposed a hefty tax on auction sales and the market swiftly moved to London. Now the EU threatens London and the market is moving again, this time to New York.

Despite strong British protests Brussels imposed an EU tax of 2.5 per cent on works of art imported into the EU for sale from 1995. In the first four years of the tax art imports to London dropped by 40 per cent. Then Brussels doubled the tax in 1999 to 5 per cent. The London market is surviving still on the strength of its world class expertise but a tax rate of 17.5 per cent or 18 per cent will certainly kill it. That will be imposed by 2004, the end of the current five year EU plan.

In 15 years time another EU tax, droit de suite, will be imposed. Auction houses, agents, and galleries will have to charge a minimum 4 per cent when art is resold which will be paid to the artist or their heirs for 70 years after the artist's death. EU insiders think that gives 15 years to persuade the Americans to adopt the same tax, so competition would be eliminated.

Perhaps by the time that tax bites there will not be much art market left in London to worry about.

EU To Tax Mortgages And Credit Cards
'UK Tax Court' At Work

Here is a law case with huge ramifications.

The First National Bank of Chicago wanted to recover VAT on its inputs from the British Customs and Excise. The European Court of Justice heard the case in 1998. Foreign exchange dealing is exempt from tax under the EU's 6th VAT Directive, but the Bank argued that the money it made from the spread between the buying and selling price of foreign exchange was like a fee to supply a service. Therefore, it should come within the scope of VAT.

This was no ordinary case.

The EU Commission was already on the look out for ways to levy VAT on financial services and gave evidence to support the Bank. The Commission even referred in evidence to a 'proposed directive' it was about to issue on identifying taxable amounts in similar circumstances. After the case was over the Commission quietly withdrew its 'proposed directive'.

The French government, which had no connection with the case whatsoever, also backed the Bank in Court. The French wanted to establish a tax principle to support the EU.

The First National Bank of Chicago won its case against Customs and Excise.

The immediate cost was to the British Treasury, which had to pay back about £300 million. The final cost will be much higher.

The case means that the EU can now tax mortgage interest, credit card transactions, and other financial instruments whenever it is politically strong enough to do so.

It will be expensive for the British. In Britain, two thirds of homes are owned, many with a mortgage, and mortgage interest can now be taxed. In the rest of the EU home ownership and mortgages are low: in Germany only 38 per cent of homes are owned.

British homeowners have higher mortgages than their continental counterparts.

The British use credit cards and store cards far more than anywhere else in the EU.

Britain and the US are both remarkably similar on home ownership and credit cards and both remarkably different to Europe.

Taxing Energy

A Draft Energy Products Directive proposes fundamental changes in energy tax in the EU, supposedly to satisfy environmental rather than fiscal objectives. Progress on the directive has been very slow.

National Customs Duties Become EU Customs Duties

Customs frontiers throughout the EU were abolished in 1993 by the Single European Act and a 1991 directive. Eventually duty free allowances on alcohol and cigarettes were abolished in 1999.

Now a pilot project, the Single European Authorisation Project, is testing a single point of customs reporting and payment system for all imports into the EU, no matter where they come in. All imports will be treated as imports into a single territory.

Customs duties will then become an EU tax.

Attacking The National Right To Tax Businesses And Individuals

> 'The EU Code of Conduct Group on business taxation has identified over 280 special regimes relating to the tax systems of EU Member States and their dependent territories, more than 60 of which qualified as 'harmful' to fair competition, because they apply a lower-than-normal tax rate to particular businesses . . .
>
> 'Without the eradication of integral tax havens (like the Channel Islands) and tax havens for certain businesses (like corporate headquarters in Belgium), progress towards fairer corporate taxation in the member states will be nearly impossible.'
>
> *Draft report on Tax reforms in Member States, Committee on Economic and Monetary Affairs, European Parliament,*
>
> *4.10.2000*

Germany wants to stop both Germans investing money outside the country to save tax, and other countries offering better tax deals to Germany's detriment. The EU wants an EU tax regime.

Germany triggered the first major EU tax crisis. In 1988, it imposed a 10 per cent withholding tax on interest from savings. As a result, £100 to £400 billion ($1.5 to $6 billion) rapidly escaped from Germany to Luxembourg. The Deutschmark, under pressure, fell sharply. Quickly Germany repealed the tax, but the problem remained. Germans were investing abroad and not declaring their income to the German tax authorities.

Germans have suffered high taxes for years. The average German surrendered half his wage packet to the government in direct, indirect taxes and social welfare contributions. The

German government's answer to tax evasion was to try to push up the overall EU tax base to its own level. Meanwhile Germany was losing about £70 billion ($105 billion) every year. Germans used to put their money in Luxembourg, next door, but then Luxembourg came under such tight German scrutiny that the money went further afield to such 'havens' as Jersey, Liechtenstein, and Switzerland. The German spotlight reached those countries too. Germany even offered cash rewards to informants who denounced suspected tax evaders.

Having failed – at least in the short term – to push up the EU's tax rates to Germany's level, the German government had to cut taxes to stop money fleeing abroad and boost the domestic economy and employment. The Tax Reduction Bill of July 2000 cut corporation tax from 40 per cent to 25 per cent from 2001 and reduced the top rate of income tax from 51 to 43 per cent.

German anxieties have taken years to translate into EU action. Although there was a proposal to 'harmonise' corporation tax as long ago as 1962 (the Sagré Committee Report), it was not until 1996 that the Commission came up with a tough tax agenda with published proposals for,

- ○ EU tax audits
- ○ A minimum withholding tax on interest paid to individuals
- ○ Environmental taxes
- ○ A minimum corporation tax of 30 per cent
- ○ A Code of Conduct on Business Tax to 'define common standards'

      Tax in the EU: Report on the Development of Tax Systems

'We must harmonise taxes . . . harmonisation of corporate taxes is the next item on the agenda.'

Yves-Thibault de Silguy, when EU Commissioner for
Economic Affairs, December 1998

'The times of individual national efforts regarding employment policies, social and tax policies are definitely over.'

Gerhard Schroder, German Chancellor, January 1999

'Member States [will] not introduce new tax measures which are harmful within the meaning of this code . . . Member States [will] re-examine their existing laws and practices, having regard to the principles underlying the code . . . Member States will amend such laws and practices . . . '

EU Code of Conduct for Business Taxation, 1997

The Code of Conduct is 'an international agreement . . . to eliminate what we see as being aggressive and unfair . . . competition . . . We expect other Member States to fulfil their political commitments as Germany is willing to do . . . '

Ulrich Wolff, German Ministry of Finance, evidence to House of
Lords Select Committee on the EU's Code of Conduct,

20.7.1999

What Is The EU Code of Conduct?

'The Code concerns "those measure which affect, or which are to be regarded as *potentially harmful* if they provide for a significantly lower effective level of taxation . . . than that which generally applies in the Member State in question;" a judgement is then made as to whether they are actually harmful with in the meaning of the Code and to amend their laws and practices as necessary with a view to eliminating any existing harmful measures as soon a possible . . .

'The process could lead to the United Kingdom being obliged – in practice if not in law – to adopt tax measures damaging to the interests of the economy or of citizens.'

House of Lords 15th Report on the European Communities,
'Taxes in the EU: Can co-ordination and competition co-exist?'
20.7.1999

Agreeing to the Code of Conduct on Business Tax is like writing a blank cheque to Brussels but all the Member States, including Britain, did so in 1997. The Code of Conduct will *permanently* co-ordinate tax policies and attack what the EU calls 'harmful tax competition', that is anything it does not like.

The Code appears to lack teeth but like most EU tactics it is Machiavellian. It says 'some of the tax measures covered by this Code may fall within the scope of the provisions on state aid in Articles 92 to 94 of the Treaty [of Rome]'. So the Single Market rules apply and there is no national veto.

A group of Ministers from each EU country began to monitor adherence to the Code in 1998. For the first two years it had a British chairman, Dawn Primorolo.

Within a year, the Commission issued the first Communication under the Code banning low company taxes 'disguised' as state aid. The group's very existence also had an immediate effect: EU countries felt obliged to limit new tax measures to conform to EU thinking.

Each country is encouraged to inform on other countries and tell the Commission about tax measures it thinks falls within the EU's Code.

The British review of the status of Britain's remaining colonies was largely decided in timing and scope by the Code's intolerance of offshore low tax areas.

The Code of Conduct Group has already made three major proposals,

- Corporation taxes are to be increased within each country so governments cannot 'provide for a significantly lower effective level of taxation . . . which is potentially harmful'
- Unless the EU gives its approval Britain will not be able to help particular sectors, like the film industry or poorer areas of the country. Gordon Brown, the Chancellor of the Exchequer, had to reject the idea of 'urban priority areas' because they fell foul of the EU Code. Of course he did not blame the EU
- One tax system for interest and royalty payments between associated companies in different Member States
- Taxing interest on savings invested in the EU by people resident in another EU country. The group suggested *either* imposing a 20 per cent withholding tax at source, *or* providing the Member State where the investor is resident for tax purposes with information about the payments so they can be taxed

EU Rules On National Tax Cuts

In February 2000 an EU Commission Report listed four criteria Member States will have to apply if they want to cut taxes from 2001 onwards:

Member States can cut taxes without making equal cuts in public spending only if their budgets are close to balance or in surplus, as defined by the EU.

Taxes and spending cuts must be done together so that taxes are not cut during times of economic growth

Governments must take account of public debt and long-term public finances.

Tax cuts should be part of a comprehensive reform package to boost output and employment.

The British government fought the withholding tax long and hard. Taxing at source has been defeated, at least for the moment. If it had been imposed funds would have immediately flowed out of London and out of the EU; the City of London would lose thousands of jobs; and all the financial markets would be seriously unsettled. That could easily mean a recession.

The only reason London today is the centre for eurobonds was that in the early 1970s the US imposed a similar tax. The flight of money from New York to London was instant.

The Institute of Directors (IoD) warned,

> 'If the EU . . . introduces a withholding tax . . . it will send out the message that the EU is not a good place in which to do this kind of business.'

Richard Baron of the IoD writing for the Centre for Policy Studies said the message would be that the British government 'is prepared to accept short-term insecure compromises.' Major financial institutions would think again about a base in London for fear of what could happen next. The jobs lost, according to many in the City, would not just be the 10,000 paying and custodial agents but 100,000 of the 600,000 employed in the City of London.

The EU countries compromised on the reporting option *provided that* non-EU countries like Switzerland, Liechtenstein and the US agreed too. That likelihood is small and the EU will now rethink its method of attack.

But according to the Swiss newspaper, *Neue Zuercher Zeitung* on 21st June 2000, the EU 'passed the hot potato to their most important partners, like Switzerland.' The newspaper warned that pressure on Swiss banking secrecy would increase because 'the EU has multiple ways to choke Bern, and could link the signature of new bilateral accords' with the tax reporting plan.

Had the Withholding Tax at source gone ahead the EU would have had a vital central clearinghouse and register of individual taxpayers and paying agents. Both are essential if the EU is to tax individuals. It is also essential for EU corporation tax.

Without a doubt those plans will be revived.

EU Attacks Tax Havens: That Means Britain Too

'Governments cannot stand back while their tax bases are eroded . . . [by] tax havens'

The OECD

The EU 'has quietly entered the operational phase of the alignment of taxation.'

The Prime Minister of Luxembourg

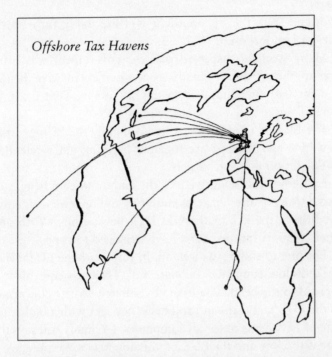

Offshore Tax Havens

The £4 to £8 trillion ($6 to $12 trillion) held in offshore tax havens, including Britain and Ireland, is the paramount EU tax target. The interest on that would provide a huge tax take for Brussels, provided of course that the money did not escape to other parts of the world. It is an extraordinary fact that nearly every significant tax haven in the world is either in the EU or a British dependency or overseas territory.

The British government said that within present constitutional arrangements it would make sure that the principles of the Code of Conduct are carried out in British Overseas Territories and Crown Dependencies. If the government succeeds it will destroy the economies of the Channel Islands, the Isle of Man, the Cayman Islands, Bermuda, and many others.

It will also hit the City of London, which manages most of the money held offshore in the Channel Islands and the Isle of Man. Then the EU spotlight will inevitably turn on the City of London itself.

Many strongly suspected that the government was offering up the offshore islands as a sacrifice to save Britain and the City of London from the tax attack. That is a false hope.

The EU and the OECD (which is mainly the EU operating as a bloc and the US) are together carrying out a relentless onslaught on the 'soft targets'.

An island representative told the author 'we are being subjected to wave after wave of enquiries and reviews – it's either the British, the EU, or the OECD. It never stops.' With only small administrations, most have struggled to cope.

The first to suffer was Ireland. In July 1998 the EU labelled Ireland's low company tax 'state aid'. That was equivalent to a pistol to the head. The Irish government swiftly conformed to the EU's 'standstill and roll back' concept with a higher tax rate of 12.5 per cent for all companies. Germany still says this rate is too low and the EU Commission may exert pressure to increase it again. No doubt that pressure will continue until eventually the Irish raise the tax to 30 per cent.

The EU held *exploratory* talks with Liechtenstein and more advanced talks with Andorra, Monaco, and San Marino. No one knows exactly what that meant but *Le Monde* helpfully reported in the autumn of 1998 that Monaco had been threatened. The French apparently told the Monegasques that if they did not toe the line their electricity supply would be cut off. Presumably that was when the talks moved smartly from the 'exploratory' category to the 'more advanced'.

Prince Rainier of Monaco told the French government in October 2000 to stop meddling in Monaco's affairs after two French parliamentary reports accused it of being a haven for money launderers and a 'non co-operative state.' It is well known that French resorts neighbouring Monaco are indeed havens for money launderers and that France is taking little action to tackle the problem.

In an interview in *Le Figaro* Prince Ranier said, 'I don't want to declare war on France, but France no longer respects us and hasn't for many months. The principality wishes to regain its full sovereignty.'

Soon after coming to power the British Labour government began a 'review' of Britain's remaining dependencies, which it published as a White Paper in March 1999 and innocently titled, *Britain and the Overseas Territories – a Modern Partnership.*

When the Foreign Office Minister, Baroness Symons, consulted them, the islands said they did not want any changes to their constitutions. They would like British passports but not at the price of British tax rates and tax regime. They would like closer ties with the British Commonwealth. No one asked them about closer ties with the EU, or gave them the chance to say no.

The White Paper proposals, if adopted, will effectively impose an EU regime: they will overturn the British dependencies legal systems and their constitutions, and destroy their ability to attract funds with low tax rates. The bribe offered to the islanders is a British passport with the right to live in Britain and use the welfare state. The passport will also mean visa-free travel throughout the EU.

The only press coverage the White Paper received in Britain was along the lines of 'righting a colonial wrong'. It is the opposite. It is a sell out.

Robin Cook, the Foreign Secretary, assured the Commons there would be no mass exodus of people from the islands to Britain because 70 per cent of the population of the overseas territories had a higher income per head than Britain. But he failed to mention that if tax competition ended the islands' financial industries would be destroyed and there might indeed be a mass exodus.

The White Paper made clear that with the British passport would come new responsibilities. The Overseas Territories were told to bring their laws on banking as well as some of their human rights practices, into line with British (that is EU) standards.

What the Foreign Secretary did not say is that a British passport will be tantamount to an EU passport, making its holder an EU citizen and open to any duties the EU may later impose.

The British government said in the White Paper that there were no proposals for a British tax regime attached to the offers of British citizenship. The government is being economical with the truth. EU, not British, taxes will be imposed.

The White Paper mentioned legal co-operation with no hint that the door will be wide open to all EU legislation. The White Paper mentioned human rights and threatened that if the Islands did not voluntarily change some of their statutes then the government would impose changes either by Order in Council or Act of Parliament as appropriate. The Paper acknowledged that 'in some of the Caribbean communities there is particularly strong opposition to homosexuality, based upon firmly held religious beliefs.' Those beliefs will be overruled at the stroke of a pen.

The Overseas Territories have been offered independence with British government help if they do not accept these terms. Unless the island governments have read between the lines they will walk straight into the trap set by the British government working with the EU. Pressure will come from their peoples who will want British passports. Everything the islands have said they do not want will then be imposed on them.

Income Tax

> 'We should create an 'own resource' for the Union
> in the form of a direct income tax, independent of
> nationality.'
>
> *Jose Maria Gil-Robles, President of*
> *the European Parliament, 24.10.1998*

There is no explicit provision in the Treaty of Rome to 'harmonise' direct taxes including income tax. The EU Commission has been seeking ways round this and has tried adding personal tax to the Code of Conduct. Under heavy fire, the EU had to withdraw but has *guaranteed* it will bring it back later.

In 1996 ECOSOC, a toothless group of 222 representatives from the so-called EU regions, showed what the EU has in mind by proposing:

- ○ 'A European resident' for tax purposes
- ○ The end of all tax havens in the EU (that would include Britain)
- ○ An EU tax on savings from financial instruments
- ○ 'Harmonise' all EU inheritance and wealth taxes because wealth is mobile
- ○ An EU tax on the income of all highly skilled and therefore mobile workers (e.g. doctors, bankers, accountants, lawyers, IT workers)
- ○ An EU income tax on people working near national borders

The EU tax attack on the nation states has only just begun, successes so far have been limited, but the onslaught is relentless and continues in the Treaty of Nice. The British government shows some signs of giving in – sacrificing the offshore islands to save the City. That would be the thin end of the wedge.

French Tax Exiles

French mayors elected the model and actress, Laetitia Casta, to embody Marianne, the symbol of France. Unfortunately she moved to London, apparently to escape high French taxes. Laetitia was accused of being a traitor and was said to be lacking in 'fiscal patriotism'.

A cartoon in *Le Figaro* showed a statue of Marianne, in a bonnet bearing a Union Jack. The legend said 'Liberté, Egalité, Fraternité', but after the word Liberté are the words 'not to be fleeced'.

Laetitia is estimated to earn 20 million francs a year. She can save 4 million by living in Britain.

The French top rate of income tax is 54 per cent, the British top rate is 40 per cent.

About 250,000 French people live in London. They may be the largest group of rich foreigners in Britain.

Chapter 9

A NATION OF SHOPKEEPERS

The Backdoor To Political Union

Despite the British government's loss of control over trade policy the British debate on the EU is couched primarily in trade terms. Why is that so? The simple answer is that it is not politically acceptable to tell the truth. The economy has always been targeted as the backdoor to political union.

'A federal union should begin as unambitiously as possible in the economic sphere . . . to secure the acceptance of those who advocate collectivism.'

Harold Wilson, when a Fellow of University College,
Oxford in 1940, later Prime Minister

'We shall avoid needless difficulties if we adopt an economic approach . . . We shall soon find . . . that economic issues cannot be separated from political and social ones . . . '

Comte Paul van Zeeland, former Belgian Prime Minister, 1945

'No government dependent upon a democratic vote could possibly agree in advance to the sacrifices, which any adequate plan must involve. The people must be led slowly and unconsciously into the abandonment of their traditional economic defences, not asked . . . to make changes of which they may not at first recognise the advantages to themselves.'

'Design for Freedom' largely written by Peter Thorneycroft MP
and endorsed by 23 others mainly Conservative, 1947. They said
they wished to preserve the 'good' Hitler had done to make
Europe one economic unit.

[The Common Market] involves a very significant
surrender of national sovereignty.
Lord Cockfield, former EU Commissioner, in
'The European Union, Creating the Single Market'

Long ago the British government ceased to have any authority over British trade – it handed that authority to Brussels.
Brussels directives and regulations are steadily overwhelming
Britain's trade, business and the City of London. If the government does not make a successful stand Britain will become
an economic satellite of the EU. It will be heavily regulated
and highly taxed to satisfy a vast array of socialist dreams
from protecting the environment to social engineering. Free
trade will be dead.

The Single Market goes far beyond trade issues. There is
scarcely an area of national life which does not bear the
imprint of Brussels' rules. Single Market legislation, with no
national veto, was used to introduce a wide range of measures such as the 48-hour working week, thus making a mock-
ery of Britain's opt out via the Social Chapter. France has
gone further with a 35-hour working week and pressure is
building to extend that to the whole EU. The Commission
has used its power over health and safety to extend its ability to legislate across the whole field of employment law.

No one likes to be fooled. Understandably perhaps the
British government under every Prime Minister from Edward
Heath to Tony Blair is coy about admitting what it has done.

Less understandably, some organisations which represent British free trading businessmen like the Confederation of British Industry (CBI) and the Institute of Directors (IoD) are equally coy about telling their memberships that the emperor has no clothes. The CBI is heavily involved in the Brussels' machine through ECOSOC (see page 272).

'Tomorrow's political unity will depend on making the economic union effective in the everyday activities of industry, agriculture, and government. Little by little the work of the Communities will be felt . . . Then, the everyday realities themselves will make it possible to form the political union which is the goal of our Community and to establish the United States of Europe.'

Jean Monnet's United States of Europe Action Committee, 1958

'We have all along recognised that the Treaties of Rome and Paris had a political as well as an economic objective.'

Edward Heath to the Council of the WEU, 1962

'The primary reason why Britain entered into these negotiations was political, political in its widest sense.'

Edward Heath, lecture at Harvard, 1967

'A decision to join the Community would be essentially a political act with economic consequences, rather than an economic act with political consequences.'

Heathcoat Amory, Chancellor of the Exchequer, 1971

The Brussels' Lobby System

The EU is now more lobby-orientated than any country in Europe.

As Brussels' power has risen over the member countries so democracy has correspondingly diminished. The lobby system has largely replaced democracy.

Brussels hands out subsidies, decrees, and regulations and can make or break businesses. Therefore businessmen flock to Brussels, often setting up permanent offices, and bypassing their national parliaments. The Brussels telephone directory reads like a *Who's Who* of world companies.

The European Round Table of Industrialists was partly founded by the EU Commissioners in 1983. The 48 largest companies in the EU, including Shell, BP, GEC and BT are one of the most powerful lobby groups in Brussels. These same companies dominate the CBI in London. That is an additional reason why the CBI leadership takes a pro-EU view while its wider membership, without a Brussels' inside track, is cynical.

The Brussels' lobby system has encouraged EU wide groups to curry favour such as:

○ Unice, the European confederation of employees
○ Eurochambres, the federation of chambers of commerce
○ AmCham, the EU Committee of the American Chambers of Commerce representing the interests of large US companies with operations in Europe

Typical of the Brussels' style of government is the Competitiveness Advisory Group set up in 1995 by the then EU President, Jacques Santer. Two years later Santer appointed three representatives from Round Table companies, three other corporate interests and three trade unionists to the Group.

Trade unions in Brussels are increasingly acting on an EU wide basis. In 1999 the Confederation of European Unions (ETUC) created a committee to negotiate wages on a pan-European basis. Officials have threatened 'cross-border sympathy action', including strikes, if their demands are not met. The British Labour Party backs collective bargaining across the EU.

The ETUC demanded an *upward convergence* of wages across the EU, standardising working conditions, a 35-hour week, and a legal guarantee of the right to strike in the next EU treaty. The leader of the five million-strong Italian Union, the CGIL, said 'The euro contract will be a reality within ten years.'

The EU's 'social' regulation and its Social Charter encourage pan-EU collective bargaining, with a generous minimum wage and high redundancy costs beckoning. EU wide strikes will be increasingly common.

Anyone who needs money or favours now goes to the new Imperial Court of Europe in Brussels, which already rivals Vienna at the height of the old Austro-Hungarian Empire.

The Enemy Of Free Trade

> Mikhail Gorbachev, the former Russian President, told his British companions over dinner at the Carlton Club in London that 'it was particularly surprising that our leaders are trying to construct a European soviet' after he, Gorbachev, had overseen the fall of the Russian one.
>
> *The Daily Telegraph, Peterborough column, 24.3.2000*

Britain is a free trading country; the EU is not. The EU is a customs union and a protectionist bloc with one central authority, one external tariff, and one trade policy. The EU replaced a number of customs borders with one single

Political Parallels	German Zollverein	The EU
Metric weights and measures enforced	√	√
Taxes 'harmonised	√	√
Nearly half of taxes spent on administration	√	√
One currency	√	√
Commercial law 'harmonised'	√	√
Uniform rules for industry and workers	√	√
Trade treaties negotiated and signed	√	√
National veto replaced by qualified majority voting	√	√
Opt outs always led to opt-ins	√	√
Big sums paid for hidden political advantage	√	√

national customs border. The four so-called freedoms – the free movement of goods, people, services, and capital – all operate within that protective wall.

That Single Market has still not been completed. The first stage of eliminating tariff barriers was achieved by the deadline of 1967. But the non-tariff barriers remained: the unification of services, transport, and tax was largely ignored. With a new deadline of 1992 the Commission began an eight-year programme to break down more national barriers. They called it the Single Market though it was just a second try at creating the Common Market.

The centrepiece of the 1985 Single European Act destroyed what remained of national independence on trade. Yet Brussels billed it as *more free trade*, which the British believed. In fact the Act abolished the national veto on all remaining trade matters.

It has all been done before. In the nineteenth century Prussia deliberately took over the 39 neighbouring German states and principalities via the economic back door. Prussia took 15 years to create a German customs union or Zollverein and a total of 48 years to reach full political union (1871), ending with three wars.

The EU is taking just a little longer to become one country. Starting with the European Coal and Steel Community of 1952 the Treaty of Nice 2000 is the sixth agreement. If it succeeds it will have taken over 50 years without, so far, recourse to war. For the full history see *Britain Held Hostage, The Coming Euro-Dictatorship*.

Does Britain need the EU?

Britain does not need the EU to survive. Britain not only loses money on trade with the other EU countries but also pays Brussels huge sums of money for the privilege of doing so.

In 1999 Britain paid Brussels £11.44 billion ($17 billion) in contributions. That is £220 million ($330 million) a week, £31 million ($47 million) every day or £1.3 million ($2 million) every hour. Every year the toll goes up and it is rising faster than both inflation and the growth of the British economy.

The Commission now talks of ending Britain's rebate negotiated by Lady Thatcher in 1984 as compensation for Britain's low share of payments from the Common

Agricultural Policy. That would at a stroke add at least £2 billion ($3 billion) to Britain's bill. In March 1999 Tony Blair defended the rebate against a concerted attack by most of the other EU countries and was forced to give ground on budget changes, which would have benefited Britain. That will no doubt be the pattern for the future and the defence of the rebate will prove expensive.

On 4th October 1999 in Berlin, Romano Prodi, President of the Commission made clear that the British rebate would almost certainly have to be scrapped by the time the first group of former Communist countries join the EU.

What does Brussels do with the British taxpayers money? Brussels keeps over 40 per cent to give to other countries and to fund its own bureaucracy. The rest is returned to Britain mainly as farm subsidies, as Brussels decrees.

That is a huge cost and a distortion of trade, which has to be justified. Does Britain's trade with the EU merit protection money?

Year after year Britain loses money on its business with the 14 other countries of the EU. It makes money from the rest of the world and from the non-EU countries of Europe, such as Switzerland and Norway. So Britain survives despite the EU not because of it. In the 1990s the US, from *outside* the EU, has increased its exports to the EU far faster than Britain has done from *inside* the EU.

o Britain's most important market is the US, both for visible and invisible exports with nearly 20 per cent of all exports, see

o In 1999 Britain invested £50 billion ($75 billion) in firms in the US compared to only £4 billion ($6 billion) in Euroland, a long-standing pattern and just part of Britain's vast global investments, which send regular dividends home

○ Between 1993 and 1999 British exports of all kinds to
the US grew faster than to anywhere else in the world.
They are growing slowest to the EU, especially to the
Euroland countries

Britain's *Apparent* Top Export Markets In 1999

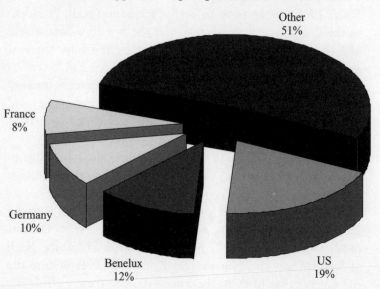

While the US is clearly Britain's key trading partner the
order of the rest of the list is cast into doubt by what is
known as the Rotterdam effect. Common sense suggests that
two small countries, Belgium and the Netherlands are unlikely to be Britain's second most important markets in the
world, but that is what the statistics suggest.

They say that about 11 per cent of Britain's GDP is export-
ed to the EU but after taking the Rotterdam effect into
account it is probably about 8 per cent.

Rotterdam: Lies, Damn Lies and Statistics

'We sell more to the Netherlands than we sell to all the Asian tiger economies.'

Stephen Byers, Secretary of State for Trade and Industry in the Financial Times, 21.2.2000

'More than half of Britain's trade is with the rest of the EU.'

The Britain in Europe campaign

Both these statements are false. In 1999 49.2 per cent of all visible and invisible exports *appeared* to go to the EU.

The statistics show that Britain exports three times more to every Dutchman and Belgian than to their German or French neighbours. It looks wrong and it is wrong.

About two thirds of British physical (or visible) exports go in sealed containers from British docks like Felixstowe to Rotterdam and Antwerp. At Rotterdam and Antwerp many of those containers are loaded onto very large container ships for ports like Singapore and Shanghai in the Far East and the Americas. Once there they may be transhipped again to smaller ports.

The statistics only show that goods go to the Netherlands and Belgium and not where they go after that.

How much does Britain really export to the EU? EU apologists regularly claim it is over half. If the Dutch and the Belgians 'consume' about the same as their French or German neighbours then the answer is probably around 35 per cent of all visible exports. No one knows exactly.

Then there are the invisibles like financial services. Britain appears to have a large investment income from the Netherlands. But with low tax the Netherlands is home to many corporate headquarters, which are no more than brass plates on the door. The true business is carried on all round the world.

A Vote Of Confidence In Britain

Britain is the number one investment destination in Europe and the second in the world after the US. Overseas businessmen do not invest in Britain because Britain is in the EU. They do so *despite* the EU. If they wanted to be in the EU they could just as logically invest in France or Germany.

Even so the significance of inward investment should not be overstated: inward investment is still only about 2 per cent of British GDP.

Companies investing in Britain *never* cite Britain's membership of the EU as a top ten reason why they do so, according to the Department of the Environment, Transport and the Regions. In the Department's regular surveys investors say they like the British work force, absence of corruption, the English language, low taxes and the lack of red tape.

The British government in the annual report for 2000 of Invest.UK said the reasons companies invest in Britain are,

- British creativity and inventiveness
- Flexible and adaptable work force
- Good labour relations
- Low tax base
- The British government's commitment to lasting economic stability
- British R and D
- An educated work force

Yet in the report the government repeated the old canard that overseas companies appreciate 'the government's desire to play its full part at the heart of the European Union.'

The US is the largest investor in Britain by far with over half of all inward investment. Japan, whose car plants are regularly featured in the press as critical for jobs and Britain's very survival, ranks not much higher than Bermuda.

Why Is The EU So Keen To Control British Trade?

> '[German] exports to Britain alone were as much as to the whole of Asia.'
>
> *A German government press release, 19.5.2000*

> 'In 1999 Britain was Germany's third largest single export market.'
>
> *A German government press release, 5.9.2000*

The other 14 countries of the EU need free access to the British market because,

- Britain is their single biggest market, bigger than the US by about 20 per cent
- They profit from a large trade surplus with Britain every year
- By investing in Britain they gain access to other English speaking markets
- They escape from their over-regulated and costly domestic markets and benefit from the much more dynamic British economy

Britain is a rich country:

- The fourth largest trading nation in the world
- Britain does more trade per head of population than any other country in the world
- In 1999 British companies invested more money around the world than any other country
- Britain is the world's largest investor in the US, dwarfing even the Japanese
- Britain attracts more investment by far than any other EU country – twice that of France and three times that of Germany

Exports Per Person In 1997

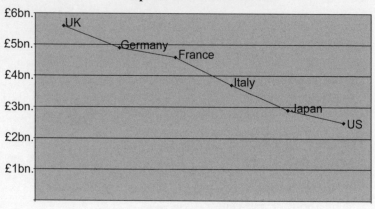

Britain's Exports In 1999

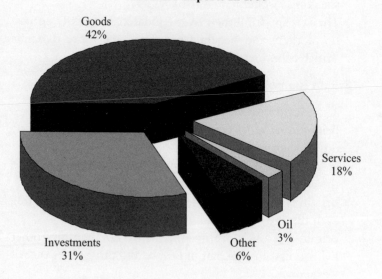

Lost: All Influence At The Top Table

> 'For all their pretence that they had a serious role to play at Seattle, it was clear that UK ministers spoke as executives of the European Union.'
>
> *Ronald Stewart-Brown, an independent observer at the Seattle WTO talks, 1999*

Despite its wealth and world class economy Britain no longer has any significant influence on the politics of world trade.

During the 1975 referendum on Britain's membership of the EEC most British people thought, and were encouraged to think, that the EEC was all about free trade. How wrong they were even then. When Britain acceded to the Treaty of Rome British freedom to regulate overseas trade began to go. At once,

- The British government's right to negotiate or sign a trade treaty ended
- The government's legal identity in trade matters outside the EU ended

Under the 1973 Treaty of Rome the British government cannot negotiate or sign *any* trade treaties. Since 1973 British businessmen have ceased to have the backing of the Foreign Office in this important area. And since 1973 the European Community has signed over 300 trade agreements with countries and trading groups worldwide *on Britain's behalf*. Often the British government is not involved at all and may not even have a copy of the trade treaty in London, as enquirers have regularly discovered.

Between October 1999 and February 2000, for example, the European Community (which has legal identity, the EU does not) signed agreements with Australia on wine, Kazakhstan on trade in steel products, Macedonia on trade in textile products and New Zealand on measures applying to trade in live animals and animal products, and on trade with South Africa.

At the World Trade Organisation talks Britain is not allowed to take part and can only be present as an observer, just like any casual passer-by. A Frenchman currently represents Britain, Pascal Lamy, the EU Trade Commissioner.

Lost: Behind A High Tariff Wall

With fanfares, barriers to trade *within* the EU are being lowered. Quietly Brussels ignores the existence of tariff ramparts against the world: that would be bad publicity. The EU is a Fortress Europe with a high tariff wall to protect its Internal Market, the very opposite of free trade.

Recent new EU members have even had to put up tariffs to join. Brussels told the Baltic States, to re-establish some of the old Soviet economic system that they had already painfully demolished to be eligible to join.

Tariff barriers ensure that EU companies try to buy raw materials from within the EU if possible. The products may not be at the lowest world price or the best product. Before joining the EEC Britain bought most of its wheat from the US. Today American wheat is too expensive with a tariff of 68 per cent and Britain buys within the EU even though the EU farm price is much higher than the US farm price.

It is no thanks at all to the EU that tariffs are as low as they are. The Word Trade Organisation (WTO) and its predecessor GATT backed strongly by the US, Canada, Australia and New Zealand among others have made sure that tariffs have fallen despite the EU.

The WTO has reduced the average tariff to 3.8 per cent and aims for zero. Zero may now be impossible. The EU's presence at WTO meetings actually *reduces* the chance of lower world tariffs because the EU operates as a bloc with an agenda which goes far beyond tariff reductions to environmental, social and other issues. And the EU is becoming stronger in world politics. Instead of focussing narrowly on key tariffs the EU tries to argue a complex agenda and brings proceedings to a standstill, as happened at Seattle in 1999.

The Walls of Fortress Europe			
Anti-dumping duties		*EU tariff*	
	%		%
Shoes	29	Beef and lamb	88
Industrial chemicals	28	Cereals	68
Iron and steel	29	Clothing	12
Leather products	23	Dairy products	58
Metal products	44	Drinks	22
Motorcycles and bicycle	28	Food products	27
Office and computing		Sugar	62
equipment	20	Tobacco	59
Printing and publishing	19		
Radio, TV and		*From The Economist,*	
communication	23	*22.5.1999*	

Lost: The Force Of Competition

The Single Market has destroyed internal EU competition. Instead of 15 governments competing for business there is now only one in Brussels. No competition means higher taxes, more regulation and fewer jobs. If the proposed enlargement to include Eastern European countries goes ahead, then more competing governments will be subsumed into one European Government.

EU apologists claim that the EU is like the US, just a federation of states. It is the exact opposite of the US. Each of the 51 American states sets its own local taxes, determines its own local regulation, has its own local laws and courts. States compete with each other to attract and keep business. Competition keeps both tax and regulation low in spite of the centralising tendencies of Washington DC.

For example, sales tax in US states varies between zero and 8 per cent. The state of New Hampshire has neither a sales nor an income tax.

In the EU the minimum sales tax – or VAT – is 15 per cent and it can be as high as 20 per cent. In Britain it is 17.5 per cent. VAT is a tax on business and a tax on jobs. Critically, because it is imposed across the EU, VAT is a tax on competition.

Lost: Britain Paid The Bill To Open Up Its Markets

> 'Why should we give away our former colonial markets for which engineering products had always been specified in Imperial units, and, by metrication, open up the vast replacement and maintenance requirements to foreign competition, at the same time causing a massive retooling operation in our own factories?'
>
> *John Murray's Memorandum to Hugh Gaitskell, leader of the Labour Party, 1962*

> 'Manufacturing in other members states [of the EU] have difficulty competing with UK manufacturers in imperial units.'
>
> *The Department of Trade and Industry, 1994*

> ' . . . the implementation of the Metric Directive 80/181 results in high costs for European businesses

exporting to the US; calls . . . for an initiative . . . to encourage the adoption of the metric system by the US.'

Erika Mann, German Social Democrat MEP in a
European Parliament report, 1998

'Manufacturers in other Member States have difficulty competing with UK manufacturers in Imperial units. For this reason alone it is unlikely that other Member States would support an extension beyond December 31st 1999.'

Department of Consumer Affairs to the British Weights
and Measures Association, 1999

When Britain was negotiating to join the EEC, most of the world's trade was carried out in imperial units. The countries of the British Empire, the Commonwealth and the US all used imperial measures. The EEC countries put pressure on Britain to change to metric units.

In an extraordinary move Britain paid for the 'privilege' of opening up its markets to foreign competition by adopting metrication. The cost to British industry has never been calculated. It might prove to be an embarrassingly large sum. Germany was the biggest winner followed by France and Italy.

Even before Britain joined the EEC in 1973 the governments of Harold Wilson (Labour) and Edward Heath (Tory) began 'harmonisation' with Brussels. They introduced:

o VAT
o The decimal currency
o The metric system to replace the imperial system

The EU declared the British imperial system 'unfair competition', just as lower tax rates have more recently been declared 'unfair competition'. In the late 1960s Australia,

New Zealand, Canada, and South Africa, believing Britain, their major market, was adopting the metric system, rapidly changed too. The lack of a national veto has progressively forced Britain to abandon its system of weights and measures. No choice of system was allowed, as had previously been the case. Now it was to be a compulsory system to be used on pain of fines and being branded as criminals.

The British were reluctant to switch systems so the EU allowed some measurements to continue until the end of 1994. The EU then forced the metric system on Britain under qualified majority voting. By then teaching in schools had had the desired effect.

The EU granted two more concessions, or derogations, from the directive for a ten-year period. The first allowed the use of imperial units for all foods and goods alongside metric; the second was a special exemption for fresh food and other goods sold loose.

From January 2000, British fresh food retailers *have* to trade in metric units. If not, they are subjected to *criminal* prosecution. Every trader had to buy new weighing machines to show metric. At the time of writing one case was pending in the courts after a strong challenge by the British Weights and Measures Association backed by the UK Independence Party under the banner of *Metric Martyrs*.

Today Brussels only allows miles for road signs; pints of milk, beer and cider; acres for land registration only; and troy ounces for precious metals. None are used by right.

Roads are the last metric-free area in Britain. The DETR wrote,

> 'We have no plans to replace directional signs and speed limit signs with metric signs until the majority of drivers have been educated in the metric system and it is considered that the benefits of

changing signs will outweigh the very substantial costs.'

The DETR should have added, 'because it does not, lose trade for our EU competition.'

The phasing out has started. Bridge heights are steadily giving way to metric. White marker posts on motorways and major roads are placed every 100 metres. Railway markers are now in metric; canal speed limits are given in kilometres per hour even when that gives an odd result like 4.316 kms per hour.

The EU urged the only remaining big bastion of Imperial units to change to metric. The American government appeared to cave in: under the 1988 Omnibus Trade Bill all federal agencies had to use metric units by 1992. Americans rebelled. Road signs in kilometres have since been taken down, and petrol stations have gone back to gallons. President Clinton declared that no more tax dollars were to be wasted on forced conversion.

The EU has not given up. The Americans were given a ten-year derogation and *told* to adopt the metric system by 2009. Bullyboy tactics have worked with the British but not with the Americans.

The EU claims that the US metrication programme has not yet been completed and British Ministers have even asserted that a US programme is underway and is accelerating. But there is no US metrication programme.

No Benefits, Just Costs

Britain is still a highly competitive world-class country. It still has significant control over the economy as distinct from trade – that is the right to mint currency, control the money supply, change interest rates, and raise taxes. Those powers too are under constant attack.

If Britain does not leave the EU its economy will finally be absorbed into the 'European' state. Costs will go up and jobs will go down. Already those costs are hurting the British economy.

This supports the British government's 1970 assessments of the economic costs and benefits when entry to the EEC was discussed which it failed to highlight,

> 'Not only are the areas of uncertainty . . . very large, but the technical problems of making a comprehensive and realistic estimate of the effects of membership are equally formidable . . . In the long term there would be the substantial cost of the Common Agricultural Policy.' No quantitative answer could be given on whether 'the dynamic effects of membership' could offset those costs.
>
> *Government White Paper, Command 4289, February 1970*

In 2000 the Institute of Directors (IoD) concluded in a comprehensive cost and benefit analysis that Britain's membership of the EU costs between £15 billion and £25 billion every year. If Britain were to adopt the euro the cost would rise to £50 billion.

The study listed no benefits.

Despite the absence of a national veto it illogically concluded,

> 'The IoD argues that the UK should fight for radical reform from within the EU . . . IoD members strongly support membership of the EU because of the trading gains it bestows. Members also support the Single Market because it is seen as an important consideration for inward investors.'
>
> *EU Membership: 'What's the Bottom Line?'*
> *IoD Policy Paper, March 2000*

Cost: Job Losses

The Single Market has not created a single new job in the 14 continental countries of the EU.

Compare that with more than 50 million *private* sector jobs created in the US over the past 30 years, an increase of 70 per cent. Most of those new jobs have been managerial and professional, not casual work.

In the same 30-year period, with about the same increase in the working population, there has been no net rise in private sector employment in the EU 14. The only increase in jobs has been in the public sector, paid for by the taxpayer.

In the six years to 1999, Britain created more jobs than all the 11 countries in Euroland combined. Since the 1992 recession the number of people in work in Britain has risen by 2.5 million.

Germany is the worst EU country for creating jobs: since 1992 more than 1.8 million people have lost their jobs. That would have been even worse but for the government sponsored building boom in the Eastern Lander.

Britain and France have almost identical populations but 4 million more people have jobs in the UK. French unemployment is at record levels. According to official figures nearly 12 per cent of the workforce are out of work, compared with 6 per cent in Britain and 4 per cent in the US. But the official French figures ignore part of the population: the real unemployment rate could even be over 20 per cent.

Tunnelling To Free Trade

150,000 French men and women have left to 'make their fortune' in Britain via the Channel Tunnel. Many small businesses have moved to Kent. Olivier Cardi moved his company employing 40 across the Channel. He commented,

'It is very simple: in France I made 400,000 francs profit a year. Here for precisely the same work I make 1.5 million.'

Britain has lower tax, simple formalities to set up company (one form and capital of £1) and to run it (one pay slip with maximum 6 lines and income tax deducted at source against 25 lines in France and a compulsory tax return).

From Le Figaro, 19.2.2000

French businesses are attracted by the tax regime here. French employers pay 20 different categories of social security including contributions for sickness, old age, accidents at work, family allowances, retirement, unemployment: these amount to 44% of gross salaries, compared with 10% that employers here pay.

Large companies like Hoover, JVC, Akai Sony and another 1,200 like them have left France for Britain.

British Management Data Foundation

Cost: EU Raids

European Anti-Trust Investigators Yesterday
Raided Banks Across Europe
The Times 21.10.1999

EC Raids Coke Bottlers
The Wall Street Journal 19.5.2000

Brussels Raids Airline Offices
The Financial Times 22.6.2000

The Commission now routinely raids companies it thinks are breaking EU competition laws. The 'dawn raids' were described as 'terrifying' by a director of a leading oil company who witnessed one.

Cost: EU Labour Laws And Welfare

The chairman of Rolls Royce said that if Britain took on all the EU labour laws he would move the entire company to the US because it would cost at least 30 per cent more for each of their 30,000 employees.

	Britain	EU
Hiring and firing	Great freedom	Tough restrictions
Bargaining on pay and conditions	Largely up to employers and employees	Mainly at national and sector level
	Few formalities	Collective agreements often extended by law
	Union influence limited	Strong union influence
	Low minimum wage	High minimum wage

The British advantages above are already being eroded by,

○ The European Works Council directive
○ The Parental and Family Leave directive
○ The Working Time directive – the 48 hour week – imposed under the Single Market with no national veto leading to costly bureaucracy
○ The minimum wage, voluntarily adopted by the Labour government

And most of the EU's expensive welfare system has yet to hit British business.

Cost: Unfunded Pensions

'The ticking time bomb under the single currency.'
William Hague, 20.5.1999

'[British tax payers] could find themselves subsidising the large unfunded pension liabilities of other Member States.'
The House of Commons Social Security Select Committee,
23.10.1996

Britain's pensions are largely funded. Despite an ageing population the British government only pays up to 5 per cent of GDP each year to fund state pensions.

Other EU countries have unfunded pensions liabilities of trillions of pounds. Private pensions are limited and state pensions are generous and funded from current tax receipts.

To continue to fund state pensions at current generous levels the payroll tax in most EU countries will have to double by 2010 and will add nearly 20 per cent to the wage bill, according to the EU. If that is either unpalatable or impractical the normal method of funding, printing money, can no longer be used because of EMU constraints.

France, Germany and Italy in particular face big tax rises. Those three countries are already paying between 10.6 per cent and 13.3 per cent of their GDPs in pensions, over twice the British level. In Germany and Italy spending is rising by over one percentage point every year.

The doomsday scenario could be that in 2040 half of all German and Italian adults would be collecting a state pension, *if there were the money to pay for it.* France's pension liabilities would be the equivalent of its entire GDP.

The EU's answer is a Single Market in pensions with no national veto. That would be a quick way to force countries like Britain, with well-funded pensions, to pay for continental pensions at a cost of at least £20,000 ($30,000) a person or £1.2 trillion ($1.8 trillion) according to the House of Commons Social Security Select Committee, 23.10.1996.

Cost: Red Tape

Brussels regulations and directives are pushing up the cost of doing business and are increasingly sounding the death knell for jobs. Regulation in Britain may already amount to 9 per cent of GDP or £80 billion ($120 billion) in 1999.

The Institute of Directors estimated that government expenditure and regulation absorbs up to half of Britain's GDP. It could get worse: in the EU the figure is more than 60 per cent.

Cost: EU Inspectors

To ensure directives are obeyed the EU no longer relies on national governments but has begun to appoint its own inspectors, adding more bureaucracy and more cost.

Red Tape From Brussels: directives and regulations

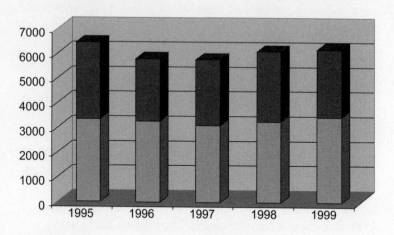

Importantly the inspectors come from other EU countries and therefore do not have ties of loyalty to the country they are inspecting. So far they inspect food operations, and plants in third countries wishing to export to the EU. EU inspectors accompany British officials and inspect all aspects of food down to the smallest country butcher. In April 2000 they produced a report critical of the British poultry sector.

The inspectors' base is in Dublin at the EU Food and Veterinary Office (FVO), set up in 1997 to carry out a regular inspection programme and produce reports on all EU food safety systems and installations.

By 1999 there were 150 EU inspectors, now increasing to 600. No doubt this growing army will soon be able to investigate other parts of British business.

In January 2000 an EU White Paper proposed that officials who discover businesses breaking EU food safety law might deduct money from EU subsidies. The inspectors will not only look but they will have powers of the purse too.

Banana Quality Control

Before 1973 and the EEC, samples of bananas were checked at the British dockside for 'stem-end' rot; and for 'pulp' temperatures to make sure the ship had followed instructions on air temperatures. Bananas are sensitive to temperature and chill can easily be spotted, the skin looks grey and the 'seeds' are black. The total inspection was three man-hours per ship for about 1,000 tonnes of bananas.

Ultimately of course the consumer was the quality control check. If he did not like the look of a banana he did not buy it.

Today under the EU it takes about 700 man-hours with twenty full time staff to do the same job in spacious laboratory style, pre-heated-examination rooms and following a huge Brussels regulations manual.

The consumer remains the ultimate judge of a banana.

Cost: 'The Single European Sky'

In June 2000 Britain gave into Franco-German demands to control all air service agreements with the US. The new European Air Safety Authority (EASA) will be an EU body and despite British pleadings non-EU countries, like the US, cannot be members. The Commission will therefore be able to bargain away very valuable slots at London airports in exchange for a few flights to the US from Marseilles.

The Commission wants an EU regulator. French air traffic controllers' have already taken strike action against the Commission's plan to change working practices forcing thousands of flight cancellations and delays.

An EU air traffic control authority is to be set up which will in due course control the movements of both civilian and military traffic, including the Royal Air Force. It will directly affect non-EU members of NATO: if for example a US plane wished to land at a US base such as Fairford permission would not come from a British authority but from the EU.

The Commission's Vice President for transport, Loyola de Palacio, said,

'It is about making borders disappear in air space that currently exist between countries and inside countries. We have to talk about a European sky, not a French, Spanish, Italian or German sky, by crossing frontiers and administrative departments which do not make much sense now.'

Cost: The Royal Mail

As eleven countries of the EU launched the euro the Royal Mail launched its first 'euro-stamp'. The new stamp which costs 30p has no price on it, just a capital E for Europe.

That was the first step towards *harmonising* postage rates – and stamps – across the EU. The navy blue stamp still bears the Queen's head, and it is unlikely that the Royal Mail will remove the Queen's head from its stamps in the near future. The monarch has been represented on every stamp published in Britain since the world's first post office was founded over 150 years ago.

The euro countries are already *harmonising* their postal rates. For the next three years their stamps will display two prices, one in the national currency and the other in euros. Eventually they will show only the euro price.

Tentative plans are being made for the first euro-stamps, with one design for all the Euroland countries.

Europost, a little heard of organisation backed by the Commission which represents 42 countries not just the 15 of the EU, meets regularly to discuss *harmonising* services. A pricing structure has already been agreed.

Senior Labour politicians have hinted strongly that their support of Britain's entry to EMU has *prompted* the Royal Mail to build links with its European counterparts.

Mark Pegg, a spokesman for the stamp dealers Stanley Gibbons, told *The Daily Telegraph* that,

> 'The Royal Mail is toeing the government line by taking us further into Europe but it could be hastening its own end as a national institution.'

The Ultimate City Take-Over

> 'Most European business leaders expect Frankfurt to overtake London as a financial centre within the next five years.'
>
> *London First, a pro-EMU campaigning group,*
> *February 1999*

> 'We need a greater centralisation of work in the European Union. I have always been of the view that central banks should regulate the financial markets.'
>
> *Wim Duisenberg, President of the European Central Bank,*
> *Argumentaire Européen, 2.6.1999*

> 'The closer integration of Europe's financial markets is crucial to our success. Without it we will not be able to exploit the economic opportunities that will underpin the Union's new competitiveness. The framework for change already exists – the Financial Services Action Plan. The speed of change in that

sector makes its implementation, by 2005, a top priority.'

Editorial, The Single Market, May 2000

The EU's greatest prize would be the take-over of the City of London, a bastion of free enterprise and the second largest financial market in the world after New York. The EU's attack on the City has recently strengthened.

At the heart of the current EU attack is the Financial Services Action Plan. By the end of the present five-year plan in 2004 the EU wants,

○ One wholesale financial market regulated by the EU
○ EU regulation of all retail financial services
○ All tax obstacles to one financial market to be abolished

In EU terminology that translates as,

'[The EU is to become] . . . the most competitive and dynamic knowledge based economy in the world capable of sustainable economic growth with more and better jobs and greater social cohesion . . . '

Presidency Conclusions, Lisbon Council, March 2000

An EU Stock Market

Mayday – Save Our Stock Exchange

Sunday Telegraph 14.5.2000

Ein Sieg für Europa (A victory for Europe)

Handelsblatt 3.5.2000

There has already been one EU inspired attempt to take-over the London Stock Exchange (LSE) and it will not be the last. The London Stock Exchange was to 'merge' with the Frankfurt Stock Exchange, to be called iX. Frankfurt would have the market in growth stocks, while glossing over the introduction of euro quotes and skating over the central issue of who was to regulate the new market. And just like the metric system when Britain paid to open up its markets, London was to pay to switch to the German settlement system.

The LSE played down the 'merger'. Don Cruickshank, chairman-designate, at first denied that one aim was to see London shares listed in euros, despite a press release saying,

> 'Subject to market conditions and consultation, the aim is for all European equity trading to be undertaken in euros.'

Members of the London Stock Exchange defeated the 'merger'. But other combinations are forming on the Continent.

The Euronext merger of Paris, Amsterdam and Brussels bourses was completed in September 2000 and the new exchange, based in Amsterdam and the second largest in Europe, was immediately rumoured to be preparing a £1.2 billion ($1.8 billion) 'friendly' take-over bid for the London Stock Exchange.

Meanwhile Deutsche Börse planned to join with the Italian and Spanish stock exchanges to bid for the London Stock Exchange. The Germans may counterbid against the £842 million ($1.26 billion) hostile bid launched on 29th August 2000 by Sweden's OM Gruppen.

Rolf Breuer, the chairman of Deutsche Börse, warned that,

> 'London does not have a system that is up to modern standards and therefore is the target for those who have availed themselves of the most modern technology. The problem has been that the British have yet to become aware of their own weakness.'
>
> *Evening Standard, 22.9.2000*

A barrage of EU directives is in preparation to create an EU financial market including,

- An EU company report and prospectus to remove barriers to raising capital across the EU
- EU laws for the securities and derivatives markets: amending the Investment Services directive, issuing a directive on market manipulation and a Communication on rules to protect investors
- An EU financial statement for listed companies in euros by amending the 4th and 7th Company Law directives
- A directive on the cross-border use of collateral in securities trades
- EU rules for cross-border company restructuring including a European Company Statute, directives on take-over bids, cross-border mergers and transfers of company headquarters and disclosure requirements to restructure the banking sector
- Fund managers will be regulated by directives on supervision and tax for supplementary pensions, and on closed-end collective investment funds

An EU Retail Financial Services Market

According to Brussels using the Internet to buy financial services will be easier with an EU bank account.

Among many directives will be distance selling of financial services, a directive on insurance intermediaries, plus a Recommendation on mortgage credit information and a plan to prevent counterfeiting and fraud in payment systems.

There cannot be one financial market without what is euphemistically called tax-co-ordination. The Commission is proposing a directive to co-ordinate tax on supplementary pensions and will remove tax distortions on financial products sold throughout the EU such as insurance and pension funds.

The EU Super Regulator

Brussels intends that the EU Securities Advisory Committee will turn into the EU Regulatory Authority, already nicknamed the EuroSec, and it will control all the present national regulators. In July 2000 a 'wise men's group' was agreed to examine the regulation of the securities markets.

There will be,

○ EU laws for banking, insurance and securities (on winding-up and liquidating banks and insurance companies, on electronic money, an amendment to the money laundering directive, amending the capital framework for banks and investment firms and amending solvency margins for insurance companies
○ A directive on the supervision of financial conglomerates

'City' Directives Already In Force	
1964	Reinsurance and retrocession Directive
1972, 1983, 1990	Motor insurance Directives
1973, 1988	Direct non-life insurance Directives
1979, 1990, 1992	Direct life assurance Directives
1985	Directive on undertakings for collective investment in transferable securities
1989, 1997	The First and Second Banking Directives
1993	Directive 93

The Soviet Europe

> 'We now have a completely united Single Market, enabling the EU to emerge as a world economic power capable of meeting the challenges of globalisation.'
>
> *Romano Prodi, President of the EU to the European Parliament, '2000-2005: Shaping the New Europe',*
>
> *15.2.2000*

The all-embracing Single Market intrudes into every nook and cranny of life and promises to invade further. All that remains on the trade front for a British government to defend is the City of London.

Chapter 10

THE EU'S LOAVES

The Luddite EU Farm Policy

'The continuation of price support (other than as a safety net) means . . . that consumers will continue to pay more than they need to for their food . . .

'Furthermore, half the gains to consumers will be offset by the taxes needed to fund the policy . . .

'The CAP . . . entrenches economic inefficiency. Subsidies to producers result in the production of goods the value of which is less than the cost of the inputs involved. This is a very poor use of taxpayers' money. The CAP also dislocates European agriculture from the rest of the world, so that trade is distorted, third countries suffer subsidised competition from the EU and EU consumers are denied goods, which they might wish to buy . . .

'The continuation of set-aside at 10 per cent is a consequence of the failure to cut support prices further.

'But it also seems that the CAP is inimical to new technology, which could improve productivity . . . '

House of Lords, 8th Report on the European Communities,
'A Reformed CAP? The outcome of Agenda 2000,' 25.5.1999

The CAP 'for which we shall have to pay so much and receive so little.'
Sir Con O'Neill, the diplomat who led Britain's negotiations to join the EEC, in Britain's Entry into the European Community, 1972

The CAP cost British consumers £6.7 billion in 1998 and taxpayers footed a further £3.4 billion to fund the scheme. The total was equivalent to £3.30 per person per week in Britain, or £250 for every man, woman and child split roughly between higher taxes and higher food prices.
Elliot Morley, Junior Agricultural Minister, Hansard, 25.11.1999

The Common Agricultural Policy (CAP) could have been dreamt up by Lewis Carroll, so *Alice in Wonderland* is it. For many years large British farms, especially arable, have benefited from it, the National Farmers Union has lobbied hard and successfully in Brussels and British farmers have 'made money' albeit at the expense of all the British.

Today depression has hit British farmers on a scale not seen since the 1930s. It is not just a case of 'the wrong crops in the wrong places at the wrong time' but subsidies paid in weakening euros via the so-called Green Pound, increased production encouraged by high prices leading in turn to low prices, and the BSE disaster. In 1998 farmers' income nearly halved. In 1999, alone, 22,000 people were forced off the land.

There are no signs that reform is at hand or that control of British agriculture might be returned to Britain. With EU enlargement to the east to include major agricultural economies like Poland, the plight of British farmers can only get worse.

The Common Agricultural Policy has been the glue holding France and Germany together. Fully operational in 1966, it guaranteed markets for French agricultural products supposedly in exchange for wider markets for German manufactured goods, but it actually guaranteed that German industry would dominate the then EEC. For over thirty years CAP has also guaranteed high food prices for inefficient farmers and huge mountains of surplus products.

All attempts to reform it have merely tinkered at the edges. French farmers and those from the poorer countries in southern Europe have a political clout far above their economic significance.

'While Australia's fruit sector has rushed to modernise and rationalise in recent years, Greek farmers who are among their main rivals still use the same techniques as their grandfathers...there is no incentive for the Europeans to change. Their governments give them whatever it takes to keep them in business.'

Mr Taylor, Chief Executive of Ardmona Foods in the Financial Times, 21.5.1999

Stalinist Style Farming

The EU Fortress Farm has a 72 per cent (1997 figures) tariff wall protecting it from the rest of the world. That compares

with the US tariff of 23 per cent and New Zealand's amaz-
ingly low tariff of 3 per cent with a profitable, nearly free
market.

The CAP is a blight on the whole world. Subsidising
European farmers and selling or giving away the EU's intervention stocks has depressed world prices. Farmers in the
Third World have been hit hard by Brussels prices with no
other options to make money.

CAP costs the world economy over £50 billion ($75 bil-
lion) a year and more than a third of that is borne by countries outside the EU mainly in the Americas, Australasia,
South-east Asia and Eastern Europe. For example, it has
cut the output of milk products in Australia and New
Zealand by more than 50 per cent. If CAP was abolished it
would save £4.2 billion ($6.3 billion) a year on just one
product, sugar, which is one of the most highly protected
of EU products. (*Global economic effects of the EU common agricultural policy; Brent Borrell and Lionel
Hubbard. Journal of the Institute of Economic Affairs, vol.
20, no 2.*)

In the 1990s the EU produced so much that it accounted
for about 30 per cent of world food exports. The EU gives
farmers subsidises of about £31 billion ($47 billion) a year.
That sustains the very many, small inefficient farms, which
are such a feature of continental Europe.

When Britain joined the Common Market in 1973 CAP
replaced the British deficiency system, which had guaranteed
a price for a product but did not disregard the market. EU
subsidies have no regard for the market price and nonsenses
of every kind abound. Britain, self-sufficient in milk, now has
to import milk and throw British milk away.

In 1999 Britain received £6.8 billion ($10.2 billion) of its
own money back in farming subsidies which then had to be
used according to Brussels diktats ignoring the market.

The Standard EU Cucumber

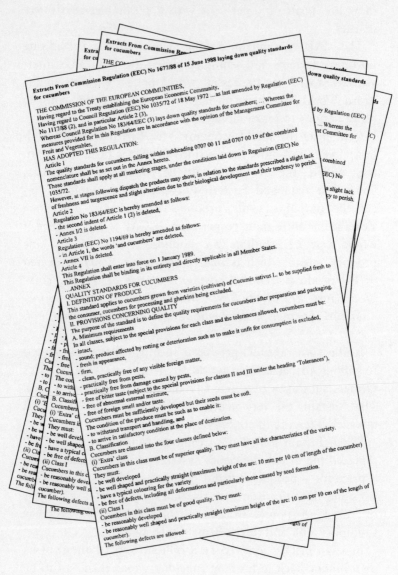

Extracts From Commission Regulation (EEC) No 1677/88 of 15 June 1988 laying down quality standards for cucumbers

THE COMMISSION OF THE EUROPEAN COMMUNITIES,
Having regard to the Treaty establishing the European Economic Community,
Having regard to Council Regulation (EEC) No 1035/72 of 18 May 1972 ...as last amended by Regulation (EEC) No 1117/88 (2), and in particular Article 2 (3),
Whereas Council Regulation No 183/64/EEC (3) lays down quality standards for cucumbers; ... Whereas the measures provided for in this Regulation are in accordance with the opinion of the Management Committee for Fruit and Vegetables,

HAS ADOPTED THIS REGULATION:

Article 1
The quality standards for cucumbers, falling within subheading 0707 00 11 and 0707 00 19 of the combined nomenclature shall be as set out in the Annex hereto.
Those standards shall apply at all marketing stages, under the conditions laid down in Regulation (EEC) No 1035/72.
However, at stages following dispatch the products may show, in relation to the standards prescribed a slight lack of freshness and turgescence and slight alteration due to their biological development and their tendency to perish.

Article 2
Regulation No 183/64/EEC is hereby amended as follows:
- the second indent of Article 1 (2) is deleted,
- Annex 1/2 is deleted.

Article 3
Regulation (EEC) No 1194/69 is hereby amended as follows:
- in Article 1, the words 'and cucumbers' are deleted,
- Annex VII is deleted.

Article 4
This Regulation shall enter into force on 1 January 1989.
This Regulation shall be binding in its entirety and directly applicable in all Member States.

...ANNEX
QUALITY STANDARDS FOR CUCUMBERS
I. DEFINITION OF PRODUCE
This standard applies to cucumbers grown from varieties (cultivars) of Cucumis sativus L. to be supplied fresh to the consumer, cucumbers for processing and gherkins being excluded.
II. PROVISIONS CONCERNING QUALITY
The purpose of the standard is to define the quality requirements for cucumbers after preparation and packaging.
A. Minimum requirements
In all classes, subject to the special provisions for each class and the tolerances allowed, cucumbers must be:
- intact,
- sound; produce affected by rotting or deterioration such as to make it unfit for consumption is excluded,
- fresh in appearance,
- firm,
- clean, practically free of any visible foreign matter,
- practically free from pests,
- practically free from damage caused by pests,
- free of bitter taste (subject to the special provisions for classes II and III under the heading 'Tolerances'),
- free of abnormal external moisture,
- free of foreign smell and/or taste.
Cucumbers must be sufficiently developed but their seeds must be soft.
The condition of the produce must be such as to enable it:
- to withstand transport and handling, and
- to arrive in satisfactory condition at the place of destination.
B. Classification
Cucumbers are classed into the four classes defined below:
(i) 'Extra' class
Cucumbers in this class must be of superior quality. They must have all the characteristics of the variety.
They must:
- be well developed
- be well shaped and practically straight (maximum height of the arc: 10 mm per 10 cm of length of the cucumber)
- have a typical colouring for the variety
- be free of defects, including all deformations and particularly those caused by seed formation.
(ii) Class I
Cucumbers in this class must be of good quality. They must:
- be reasonably developed
- be reasonably well shaped and practically straight (maximum height of the arc: 10 mm per 10 cm of the length of cucumber).
The following defects are allowed:

Britain has no control over any part of the farming process. Nor has any part of the British landscape escaped the diktats of the EU from grubbed up hedgerows, to vast fields of bright yellow rape, to empty fields where farmers are paid to do nothing. One farmer even used his set-aside funds to sponsor an archaeological dig.

Excessive and mind numbing regulations cover every aspect of farming. For example, in a mere 2000 words – the length of a very long feature article in a Sunday paper – the EU defines the look of a cucumber, the Classic Cucumber Curvature Regulation. And the bureaucrats, who may have never seen a farm, have described every fruit, every vegetable in minute and ridiculous detail. Cows have been given eartags and passports and can be tracked by satellite. Now 43 million sheep in Britain are to be eartagged.

Dr. Fischler's Rosy View of Farming

' . . . WTO negotiations cannot just centre around an automatic dismantling of customs duties and trade barriers. Basic social rights, environmental and health standards, cultural diversity and quality of life are all issues coming more and more to the fore . . .

'It is precisely these issues that society really wants to see addressed . . .

'The European model of agriculture based on multi-functional farming specifically addresses these issues and thus offers a more future-oriented perspective than mechanical calls for a total liberalisation of farm trade.'

Dr. Franz Fischler, European Commissioner for Agriculture, Rural Development and Fisheries speaking on 'CAP at the dawn of the 21st century', Berlin, 13.1.2000

'Every perceived *problem* is solved by even more inter-ference . . . greater bureaucracy, higher costs . . . a regime where the centre (Brussels) effectively tells the farmer what he may grow, in what quantities, to what standard and, to a degree, at what price. After 25 years within the CAP, we have now reached the situation in which there is, for the average family farm, hardly one aspect of British agriculture that is commercially viable . . .

' . . . farmers have been encouraged to produce for a market which in many cases simply does not exist, the most glaring example being the production of fourth-rate tobacco in southern Europe which nobody can smoke at an annual cost to the taxpayer of close on £1 billion a year . . .

'I see an industry brought to its knees by the ruinous policies of the CAP. I see a breed of independent entre-preneurs forced into a bureaucratic straitjacket, which pays no regard to the realities of the market. I see the yeomen of England and the owners of businesses in ancillary industries being forced to close . . . [by a] regime which is devoid of common sense and any vestige of morality. Repatriation of control over our own agri-culture is a vital social, economic and practical necessity for the survival of our rural areas . . . '

Christopher Gill, MP, a farmer, President of the British Pig
Association and the Meat Training Council in Farmers' Weekly,
October 1999

The Food Czars

An EU White Paper on the safety of food, *The Farm to Table Action Programme* published in January 2000, promises to introduce a maze of expensive regulation to rival or even exceed that of the CAP plus a new European Food Authority. It should be operational in 2002 and it may take another two years for the 800 pages of regulations to pass into national law.

The excuse for the new regulations was the food scares, especially BSE in cattle, the dioxin scare and an outbreak of listeria in France.

All national food agencies, like the British Food Standards Agency (FSA) launched in 2000, will be subordinate to the EU agency. The British taxpayer is already paying £110 million ($165 million) every year to fund the British FSA and the food industry another £40 million ($60 million).

The new food regulations will probably cost over £700 million ($1.05 billion) to implement in Britain alone. The most expensive change will be to record all food ingredients used in the food chain. That means that everyone in the chain will have to be registered including every food grower, producer, processor and retailer. In Britain that will mean about 600,000 businesses including restaurants, food processors, farm shops, greengrocers, ice cream vans, and sandwich bars.

Each business will have a registration number, which must appear on every individual food item from the farm to the consumer. Each outlet will have to maintain detailed records of sources. That will generate a mountain of records and expense.

To start with each country will continue to vet the system. Eventually the food agency will be able to sanction violators.

The Commission will carry out the agency's recommendations and draft more legislation. The British government has no national veto over health and safety directives, and so will not be able to stop a wave, a *tsunami* of regulations overwhelming daily life.

What is certain is that the price of food will go up and taxes will rise: the consumer will be caught both ways and will pay dearly.

Entrenched Fraud

In a system in which subsidies are at least as important as the crop grown or animals herded, fraud is endemic. The EU's Court of Auditors reported in 1997 that the EU 'lost' nearly £3 billion ($4.5 billion) through fraud, bungling and lax controls. More than £2 billion ($3 billion) went into the pockets of cereal farmers, whose subsidies remained unchanged even though world prices rose far above the level of payment guaranteed by the EU. Beef and veal farmers were overcompensated by £540 million ($810 million), again because the regulations did not allow for premiums to be lowered when market prices proved to be higher than forecast.

EU flax subsidies are worth four or five times cereal subsidies because they are meant for high-grade flax used to make linen. The Spanish flax crop, the biggest in Europe, is mainly low-grade flax with no commercial market and is grown – if it is really grown– simply to get a subsidy of £500 ($750) a hectare. According to the EU Court of Auditors, one of the largest Spanish flax producers 'harvested' nearly £1.3 million ($2 million) in EU flax subsidies over three years. Both farmers and staff from the Spanish agricultural ministry were probably guilty. More than 80 per cent of Spain's 1999 flax crop mysteriously disappeared, some of it burnt in a rash of fires.

In 1994 the EU stopped subsidies for northern Corsica because figures from Corsica's cattle owners did not add up. The catalogue of cheating filled eight pages and five annexes.

The inspectors' found that Corsican farmers,

○ Claimed livestock compensation for 1,200 cattle found feeding in lowland pastures

- Increased the number of hectares of grazing land by over half in just four years
- Mountain 'pastures' were often just rocks or bare outcrops
- One 'farmer' turned out to be a nightclub worker who had spent the year in prison

Sources: The European Parliament Summary of the First Report on Allegations regarding Fraud, Mismanagement and Nepotism in the European Commission (15.3.1999) and reports of the Court of Auditors

No Hope?

Sir Con O'Neill was right when he wrote in his 1972 report that Britain 'would receive so little' for its money. British farming, by far the most efficient in Europe and one of the most efficient in the world, is now in a desperate plight. It has been driven there not by the market nor by British incompetence but by the Brussels' bureaucracy. The one certainty is that Brussels will do nothing to help and so far nor has the British government.

An Anonymous Letter

To The Honourable Secretary of State for Agriculture
Ministry of Agriculture
Westminster

Dear Sir,
My friend, in farming at the moment, received a check for £3,000 from the government for not raising pigs. So, I want to go into the 'not raising pigs' business next year.

What I want to know is, in your opinion, what is the best kind of farm not to raise pigs on, and what is the best breed of pigs not to raise? I want to be sure that I approach this endeavour in keeping with all government policies as

---

dictated by the European Union under the CAP. I would prefer not to raise bacon pigs, but if that is not a good breed not to raise, then I will just as gladly not raise Yorkshires or Gloucester Spots.

As I see it, the hardest part of this program will be in keeping an accurate inventory of how many pigs I haven't raised.

My friend is very joyful about the future of the business. He has been raising pigs for twenty years or so, and the best he ever made on them was £1,422 in 1968, until this year when he got your check for £3,000 for not raising pigs.

If I get £3,000 for not raising 50 pigs, will I get £6,000 for not raising 100 pigs? I plan to operate on a small scale at first, holding myself down to about 4,000 pigs not raised, which will mean about £240,000 the first year. Then I can afford an aeroplane.

Now another thing, these pigs I will not raise will not eat 100,000 bushels of corn. I understand that you also pay farmers for not raising corn and wheat. Will I qualify for payments for not raising wheat and corn not to feed the 4,000 pigs I am not going to raise?

Also, I am considering the 'not milking cows' business, so send me any information you have on that too. Also please can I have the government propaganda on set aside, what is the maximum amount of land one can set aside and can this be done on an 'e-commerce' basis on virtual reality land?

In view of these circumstances, you understand that I will be totally unemployed, and plan to file for unemployment and full benefits.

Be assured I will consider you having my vote in the next election.

Yours faithfully,

A.N. Other

Chapter 11

AND THE EU'S FISHES

*From midnight on 31st December 1999 I have been
subject to constant satellite surveillance. Every two
hours my position on the planet has been transmit-
ted to the Government. I must meet all the installa-
tion and cost of transmission. What have I done to
warrant this electronic tagging? . . . My crime? I am
a fisherman, a so-called 'enemy of the environment'!*

*In 30 years at sea I have never caught a whale,
destroyed a dolphin, killed a seal or dumped nuclear
waste, but I have been forced by the EU to dump
hundreds of tonnes of edible fish in the name of
'euro-conservation' CFP style.*

George Stephen of Aberdeenshire, April 2000,
www.savebritfish.org.uk

When the four countries with the best fish resource in Europe
applied to join the EEC, the six existing members decided to
take their share of the rich pickings. Rapidly they wrote a
clause into the Treaty of Rome to make all fishing grounds
open to all EEC fishing boats.

The British Minister in charge of fishing, Jim Prior, assured
MPs that British fishing was safe. But the Prime Minister,
Edward Heath was determined to join the Common Market
by the deadline of the end of 1971 and he deliberately surrendered British fishing.

The British, Danish, and Irish all lost their fishing grounds to the EEC: only Norway realised what was afoot and voted not to join.

Transitional arrangements gave Britain ten years before the full effect of the Common Fisheries Policy (CFP) took effect. The terms were not fully fixed before Britain joined: the British Parliament agreed to a blank cheque. After ten years the British government knew the national veto would be gone and Britain could be outvoted. Every other country had an interest in making sure that the former British waters were open to all.

Britain's chief negotiator, Geoffrey Rippon, told the House of Commons in December 1971 that,

> 'It is clear that we retain full jurisdiction over the whole of our coastal waters up to twelve miles. Secondly, access to our coastal waters within six miles from our baseline is limited exclusively to British vessels. Next, in areas between six and twelve miles, where the baselines are not in them- selves a sufficient safeguard or where the stocks are already fully exploited, the fishing will also be lim- ited to British vessels and to those with existing rights to fish there for certain species of fish.'

Rippon implied to the House of Commons that Britain could use its veto to renew the derogation after ten years. The House of Lords was told *explicitly* that Britain had a veto.

In 1986 a bad situation was made worse by Spain's entry to the EEC with its enormous fishing fleets, nearly as big as all the rest put together. The former 'British' waters, supply- ing about 75 per cent of all EEC fish, were now in grave dan- ger of being over-fished. So Brussels introduced fish quotas and cut fleet sizes. That hit the British fishermen the hardest.

The Spanish were told that they would have to wait until 2003 to be fully part of the CFP. To evade the rules they started to fly the British flag ('quota hopping'). The British Parliament banned 'quota hopping' and was overruled by the European Court of Justice in 1991.

Spain threatened to veto the membership of four more countries if they were not given full fishing rights by 1996 and its bullying succeeded.

The quota system is evil. Fishermen have to dump dead fish overboard rather than land them if they have exceeded their quotas. That can sometimes be 40 per cent of their catch. Quotas cannot be properly policed and have inevitably led to violence at sea and substantial evasion of the rules.

Dumping dead fish is the opposite of environmentally sound policies. No wonder the breeding stock is falling. Subsidies are now mandatory for boats to be decommissioned. Valuable boats have to be physically broken up on the seashore under the eyes of an inspector.

The Mediterranean countries of the EU hold a blocking vote and no change is possible without their agreement. They dominate the fisheries committee of the European Parliament.

In December 1999 the EU ordered the biggest quota cut for years. Again Britain was hardest hit.

From the end of 2002, when the present derogations run out, Brussels will be able to control every aspect of European fishing including British waters right up to the beach, because even the six-mile limit will go. Even a fisherman on the beach may be infringing Brussels' rules.

Mick Mahon, a fishing skipper from Newlyn in Cornwall, wrote on 24th October 2000,

'Yesterday five Spanish fishing vessels, 16 crew each and 100 feet LOA [length overall] arrived in Newlyn.

Some of these vessels were involved four or five years ago in ripping the nets of the Newlyn fishing fleet, which was out tuna fishing.

Brussels has given these vessels 600,000 euros (£380,000 or $570,000) for two months 'research' into the fishing of anchovies, pilchards, bream, John Dory and assorted non pressure stocks of fish.

If successful, next year between 15 and 25 ships will be based in Newlyn and, if this is successful, we can look forward to a fleet of several hundred.

With the past track record the Spanish will wipe the seas clean of these fish as they have done so successfully before.

This is due to the 800 displaced Spanish boats that were removed from Moroccan waters and therefore the Spanish needed somewhere to fish.'

The 15 British armed and ageing fisheries protection vessels under the command of the Royal Navy, which police British waters, are almost certain to be replaced by EU gun boats. Britain has no plans to replace its vessels; the EU will be taking over from the Royal Navy.

Then there will only be one fishing fleet, the EU fleet, controlled by Brussels. Those British villages dependent on fishing will lose their livelihoods. So far over 25,000 British fishermen have lost their jobs because of the Brussels' fishing policy. Every man at sea supports at least another six jobs on land. Over 150,000 jobs have gone so far. And the price of fish has rocketed. Today British fishermen land only 13 per cent of all fish from 'British' waters. After 2002 that will plummet.

The remaining 18,000 British fishermen are truly an endangered species and so are Britain's fish.

Chapter 12

CREATING THE SUPERSTRUCTURE
FOR A SUPERSTATE

Power Without Accountability

The People's Europe

All these are symbols. They have no authority because the
European Union does not yet have legal identity. When it does
the Union Jack, the British national anthem and British nationality will become symbols with no meaning.

The Committee for a People's Europe created some of these
symbols in 1984 to promote a greater 'European consciousness'.

EU Flag

EU Motto

'Unity through diversity'

EU Notes and Coins

EU Anthem

Beethoven's Ninth Symphony: Ode To Joy

EU Passport

EU Driving Licence and ID Card

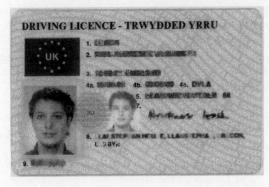

Driving Licences, ID Cards And Passports

In July 1998 the first photocard driving licences in Britain were introduced under EU Directive 96/47. Documents to accompany the application for the new driving licences changed significantly.

Under the old British rules a verified photocopy of a passport or birth certificate was all that was needed. Today under the new EU rules the *original* full current passport or birth certificate is mandatory, with a photograph certified by an MP, JP or doctor, just like an application for a passport.

The EU driving licences are the ID of the future and will be used within the EU instead of a passport. Although ID cards are widespread on the Continent, they have not been used in Britain since the wartime scheme was scrapped in 1952.

To counter fraud says the EU, light blue EU passports will be issued in 2005 with an EU ring of stars on the cover. The Royal Crest on the 'British' passport will be consigned to history. The last truly British passport, dark blue and more substantial than the EU variety, was abolished in 1988.

An EU Remembrance Day

The German Chancellor, Gerhard Schroder, may promote a Europewide 'Memorial Day' mentioning neither defeat nor victory in the world wars to replace Remembrance Day.

The Charlemagne Prize

The prize, first presented in 1950 in Charlemagne's capital of Aachen where he was buried in 814, recognises 'an outstanding contribution towards European unification'. It is in memory of the man who, like others before and since, created an empire by war, terror and what today is called 'ethnic cleansing'. Charlemagne's empire roughly equalled the land area of the six founder members of the present EU.

Recent winners were:

1992 Jacques Delors	1997 Dr. Roman Herzog
1993 Felipe González	1998 Dr. Bronislaw Geremek
1994 Gro Harlem Brundtlandt	1999 Tony Blair
1995 Dr. Franz Vranitzky	2000 President Clinton
1996 Queen Beatrix of the Netherlands	

If we are to meet this historic challenge, we must put into place the last brick in the building of European integration, namely political integration.

Joschka Fischer, German Foreign Minister, 12.5.2000

Europe needs to project its model of society into the wider world . . . We have forged a model of development and continental integration based on the principles of democracy, freedom and solidarity and it is a model that works. A model of a consensual pooling of sovereignty in which everyone of us accepts to belong to a minority . . . we must aim to become a global civil power at the service of sustainable global development then Europe will guarantee its own strategic security.

President Romano Prodi, speech to the European Parliament on Shaping the New Europe, 15.2.2000

The New Rulers Of Europe

There are two schools of thought among enthusiasts for the European Union: those who want a centralised superstate and those who prefer a federal state in which power is devolved from the centre through tiers to local authorities. All British governments have believed that power in the EU is indeed devolved and they have assured the voters of it. The

The German National Interest
An Internal Party Policy Paper

Dr. Schäuble and Karl Lamers of the CDU/CSU backed the EU, from a new constitution to an EU foreign policy and EU defence,

'Germany has always defended its national interests – without constantly using the term – and has been exceptionally successful, for some indeed too successful, in doing so. Its success has stemmed from its ability – embodied most recently by Helmut Kohl – to give its fundamental, long-term interests precedence over short-term interests. Germany must not lose this ability . . .

'And Germany, too, can be proud since it has made a significant contribution to this forward-looking project: the wisdom it showed in driving the process of European integration forward, and the benefits it has itself derived from successful integration, are reason enough for Germany to feel assured and self-confident. There is no need for Germany to adopt a new, swaggering style in its policy on Europe, especially since this would only make defence of German interests more difficult.

'Viewed in this light, Europe is the organisational framework for adjusting national policies to our continent's supranational reality, by means of a process, which ensures that the disadvantages of uncoordinated action by mutually dependent nations are avoided . . . '

Dr. Wolfgang Schäuble, CDU chairman, and Karl Lamers,
Foreign Policy Spokesman, opposition Parliamentary Group,
German Bundestag, Reflections on European Policy II – the
Future Course of European Integration, 1998

Labour government under Tony Blair (from 1997) is the most enthusiastic supporter since the Heath government (1970 to 1974).

There is no sign today, nor has there ever been, that any form of devolution has taken place or is planned. On the contrary, where the EU has power it is already highly centralised.

Germany, since the treaty of Elysée with France in 1963, has been the main engine of centralisation (see page 79). A number of smaller countries surrounding Germany, and with little choice, have usually backed the Franco-German axis, as has Italy. The Commission follows the Franco-German lead.

The political class of Brussels and local EU politicians at all levels down to the sub-regions, are well rewarded and difficult to dislodge. Proportional representation and coalitions ensure that they are unlikely to face the chilly winds of electoral change.

Civil servants, highly politicised in a way alien to Britain, are entrenched at the Brussels' trough. None are likely to vote in favour of less government, lower spending or national, let alone local, control and certainly not for democracy.

Not surprisingly, corruption is endemic and there is little incentive to root it out. In 1999 the whole Commission resigned because of corruption scandals but remained in power for several more months: some Commissioners are still in office. Former Chancellor Kohl of Germany and ex-President Mitterand of France were charged with corruption which conveniently did not surface while they were in power. Members of Forza Italia, Italy's biggest Party hold key posts on the EU Parliament's TV and Mass Media Commission and on the Justice Commission. The Party is led by Italy's richest man, Silvio Berlusconi, the subject of Italian corruption investigations, who owns three out of the four major private Italian TV national networks and is close to Italy's Fascists.

The Hard Core Of The EU

'The process of EU enlargement will soon highlight the need to find a mechanism to ease the conflict between deepening and widening, and between flexibility and cohesion. Today, even more so than four years ago, we are convinced that the concept of a *solid* – not a *hard* – core is correct . . .

'Our observation that Germany and France form the *core of the core* has likewise been fully confirmed by developments in recent years – also, indeed, by the fact that progress has slowed, and sometimes come to a halt, as a result of insufficient co-operation between these two countries. For this reason, we are concerned that some of the positions and attitudes adopted by the present Federal government display a basic misunderstanding of French (self-) perceptions: e.g. on the issue of civil or military use of nuclear energy, the political importance of agriculture, or the significance of recent history.

'There has also been a repeated lack of consensus between France and Germany not only on economic policy but also on the role of Europe in the world, its relationship to the USA, and the shaping of a European defence identity.

'In view of enlargement, we urgently need a genuine Franco-German dialogue on these problems aimed at forging a lasting consensus on the future of the European Union in particular, and, not least, on a European constitutional treaty. France and Germany must pull together to ensure that our continent stays together.'

Dr. Wolfgang Schäuble and Karl Lamers of the CDU/CSU, 1998

The Engine Within

As the EU has expanded both in numbers of countries and in its control of national governments, laggard countries appeared. Britain was the worst laggard, though not alone. To forge political union quickly an inner core of countries was essential.

In the first 50 years of integration it was easy to disguise what was really happening beneath an economic cloak. But once business inspectors, the police and the armed forces began to be combined into multinational units, with one justice system including local EU courts, then disguise of purpose would be difficult. Local opposition could become vociferous and even imperil the enterprise.

Today, the EU is poised at this critical stage.

Treaties every four to five years, with the next in 2004, can only exacerbate the problem of carrying all the nation states quietly along to the final destination of one unified country in which they will all cease to exist.

The phrase 'enhanced co-operation', a euphemism for an inner group, first appeared in the 1997 Amsterdam Treaty. Ground rules were included in the Nice Treaty for eight countries or more to accelerate to full integration. France and Germany lead the commitment to full union, they say by 2010. Other countries likely to form the inner core are the Benelux three, plus Italy, Spain and Portugal.

In the Nice Treaty the Single Market was excluded from the fast integration track. But it did include,

○ Foreign policy
○ Policing
○ Criminal justice system
○ Preventing racism and xenophobia

The European President And His Government

'The Commission is a lynchpin of the Union's institutional system. It is the guardian of the Treaties, required to act completely independently in the general interest, and . . . it has a right of initiative which is exclusive in Community matters, but shared in other areas . . . there is a general consensus that in an enlarged Union there will be a need to maintain and build upon the Commission's legitimacy and efficiency and its credibility in the eyes of the public . . . '

EU Presidency Report to the Feira Council, 14.6.2000

The Key Community Institutions

The Commission
The European Court of Justice
The European Parliament

(The Council of Ministers)

The government of the EU, though not yet in name, is the Commission or 'college' in Brussels. At the heart of that government is the tension between the Commission and the only institution representing the nation states against the centrifugal power of the EU, the Council of Ministers. Steadily, most nation states are losing their powers to the Commission, as qualified majority voting increases treaty by treaty.

A German View Of Britain

'The European Union is on the brink of becoming a European federation by the year 2010 although this Europe would not be a purely federal state. I expect no opposition from Britain. Mr. Blair signalled in his Warsaw speech earlier this month that he wants to participate in shaping Europe and he is a convinced European. But we have to be realistic. Naturally Mr. Blair has to work under certain given conditions. A British Prime Minister who declared himself in favour of federation would create huge problems for himself at home. Nonetheless I feel sure Britain will fall into line. It is a fact that Britain has always made its decision on a pragmatic basis when the pragmatic reasons for a positive step have predominated.'

Joschka Fischer, the German Foreign Minister, 16.10.2000

As Dr. Schäuble and Karl Lamers of Germany wrote in a CDU/CSU paper in 1998,

> 'It is therefore necessary and legitimate for participating countries to take part in each other's domestic debate on this issue: it is not interference in their *internal affairs*, of which the number is in any case constantly diminishing.'

Every treaty from Rome onwards has expanded the rights of the Commission at the expense of the nation state. The Inter-Governmental Conference preparing for the Nice Treaty published a list of thirty-nine more areas likely to move from the preserve of countries and said 'some of them touch upon areas of great political sensitivity',

The EU Commissioners

20 Commissioners are nominated by their countries and confirmed by the European Parliament. Their terms of office are five years renewable.

Once in Brussels Commissioners are independent of the government, which appointed them, or in the words of Lady Thatcher, 'they go native'. Commissioners swear before the Court of Justice in Luxembourg, 'To perform my duties in complete independence, in the general interest of the Communities; in carrying out my duties, neither to seek, nor to take, instruction from any government or body; to refrain from any action incompatible with my duties.' (Article 157, Treaty of Rome)

The Commission has 24 Directorate Generals, which cover every area of former national life.

Commission representatives work in every EU capital, usually from another nation.

- Foreign policy: appointing special representatives and negotiating international agreements where the terms have already been agreed by a qualified majority
- Combating discrimination
- Visas, immigration, work permits, asylum, refugees
- Rules on sea and air transport
- Removing remaining national laws and rules on the Common Market
- Incentives to promote culture 'bringing the common cultural heritage to the fore'
- Increasing industrial competitiveness
- Economic aid to poorer areas
- Rules for the overseas territories of Denmark, France, the Netherlands and Britain
- More EU agencies, with legal personality, to make the internal market work

Eurocrats Plus

The 29,000 or more civil servants, mainly in Brussels, further the Commission's aims. They are still not enough to run a bureaucratic empire. When plans were laid for the present EU in the late 1940s the College of Bruges solved the problem of a massive central bureaucracy. The College proposed a take-over of national civil services.

This clever scheme meant that national opposition would not be aroused. From the outside everything would look the same, but inside government buildings civil servants would effectively have two masters, the national government and Brussels. Civil servants were encouraged to take part in Brussels committees to acquire the Brussels' mindset.

The Brussels committee system, or Comitology, has subverted democracy. A Lords' Select committee deplored that,

Brussels' Committees
In 1997

UK Civil Service Department	Number Of EU Committees
Department of the Environment, Transport and the Regions	50
Office of National Statistics	3
Office of Science and Technology	16
Ministry of Agriculture, Fisheries and Food	48
Customs and Excise	24
Home Office	4
Department of Trade and Industry	44
Department for Education and Employment	9
Treasury	3
Health and Safety Executive	5
Cabinet Office	1
Department for International Development	8
Department of Health	6
Department of Forestry for Great Britain	1
ECGD	1
Department for Culture, Media and Sport	5
Foreign and Commonwealth Office	28

Principally derived from House of Lords Select Committee on European Communities 3rd Report, 'Delegation Of Powers To The Commission: Reforming Comitology,' 2.2.1999

The Power of the Unelected Civil Servant

'The treaties establishing the European Community . . . do not provide that all law-making is vested in the Council. In practice the Commission is frequently given implementing powers. The exercise of those powers is overseen by committees of national representatives (usually civil servants). The Council itself is rarely involved. This happens only when there is disagreement between a committee and the Commission. The European Parliament has no formal role in the process . . .

'*Comitology* is established Community shorthand for the system of procedures involving committees, chaired by the Commission. The fact that these committees exist is fairly well-known. But who sits on them, when they meet, how they work and what they decide is something of a mystery, except to insiders, assiduous Brussels watchers and a few academics and students . . .

' . . . There is, in our view, an overwhelming case for greater transparency . . . The present system is shrouded in mystery and secrecy. It is true that the existence of comitology committees is not hidden, in the sense that each committee owes its existence to a particular piece of Community primary legislation. Particular sectors of agriculture or industry may be alert to the activities of committees affecting their business. The individual citizen, however, is left very much in the dark.

'It is remarkable that not even the Commission can provide an exact number of comitology committees . . . there seems to be general agreement that there are *about* 250. But there is no up-to-date, comprehensive and easily accessible list of all the committees. That is not something in which the Commission can take any pride or comfort.'

House of Lords Select Committee on European Communities
3rd Report, 'Delegation Of Powers To The Commission:
Reforming Comitology,' 2.2.1999

The European Parliament

The treaty establishing the European Coal and Steel Community in 1951 set up the European Parliament. Its members were nominated until 1979 when the first elections were held. The constituencies are very large, divorcing MEPs from their constituents.

626 members of the European Parliament (MEPs) are elected in EU wide elections, by proportional representation, every five years (87 are British, nearly 14 per cent). A ceiling has been set on the number of MEPs at 700, so as the EU expands each MEP will serve a larger and larger constituency and become even more divorced from constituents. MEPs have diplomatic status outside their own countries.

About a third of MEPs are former national ministers: governments often send those regarded as politically dispensable to Brussels. Others have been senior diplomats or international civil servants. The trend is now towards more politicians and former MEPs.

'In most cases the only scrutiny of the Commission's implementing measures is that undertaken by national civil servants in the Comitology commit-tees. In practice there is little action in European or national parliaments . . . '

> *House of Lords Select Committee on European*
> *Communities 3rd Report, 'Delegation Of Powers To The*
> *Commission: Reforming Comitology,' 2.2.1999*

Today the 250 or more EU committees have a strong influence on the way every country is governed, especially in trade and foreign affairs. Out of the public eye national civil servants horse-trade their way to consensus positions on sub-jects of which their mastery may be limited or non-existent: it is a dark area.

The European Parliament And Its European Parties

'Political parties at European level are important as a factor for integration within the Union. They con-tribute to forming a European awareness and to ex-pressing the political will of the citizens of the Union.'

> *Article 191, Treaty of Rome*

'MEPs have an important say in a wide range of Community legislation that has a direct effect on citizens of the Union.'

> *Conservatives in the European Parliament,*
> *www.conservative-party.org.uk/ee/work.html*

In the European Parliament democracy is conspicuous by its absence. The Parliament has virtually no powers: it fol-lows the Latin tradition of legitimising the decisions of the executive. It has no similarity with parliaments based on the Westminster principle such as the British and Commonwealth parliaments or indeed the US Congress.

EU Political Parties

MEPs sit in political groups and there are two major parties, the Socialists and the Christian Democrats.

Party of European Socialists (PES): Socialist party leaders, in and out of government and Socialist Commissioners meet under the auspices of the PES several times a year to co-ordinate their positions. The British Labour Party is a member.

European People's Party (EPP): mainly Christian Democrats, similar to moderate members of the Labour party in Britain and their allies, mainly Conservative MEPs with associate status.

Other parties of roughly equal size:
European Liberal Democrat and Reform Party (ELDR): mainly Liberal parties

United European Left (GUE): mainly Communist MEPs from Italy, Greece and France and left wingers from Scandinavia.

The Green Group

European Radical Alliance: regional parities like Scottish Nationalists.

Europe of the Nations (EN): mainly French and Danish anti-Maastricht MEPs.

Independents

All major decisions are decided by deals between the leaders of the party groups. MEPs cannot initiate or repeal legislation; they can only amend or reject proposals submitted by the Commission. They can ask any number of written questions and a very limited number of oral questions. Exceptionally, MEPs can bring an action in the European Court of Justice against the Commission or the Council for failing to act.

Parliament is like a mediaeval court: MEPs and their offices are constantly on the move. They sit in Strasbourg for one week out of four and in Brussels for another week where the 20 standing committees meet. All MEPs are members of a committee. The secretariat is divided between Brussels and Luxembourg. Absenteeism is high and exacerbated by the peripatetic nature of the Parliament.

An MEP's role is frustrated by the highly technical nature of most of his work as the EU extends its remit into the smallest nook and cranny of every day life.

The time an MEP may speak in debates is allocated among the party groups according to the numbers in each group. A member of a small party, like the UK Independence Party, has only one and half minutes to make his point before his microphone is cut off.

The Commission proposes and MEPs vote following numbers on a list by pressing a button 100 to 300 times in an hour, allowing perhaps ten seconds for each vote. MEPs have trouble trying to follow the voting list, which will only have been available for a few hours and is published in French. An absent MEP is taken to have voted for the motion.

Mistakes are easily made: some Tory MEPs, voting 300 times in a two-hour session, inadvertently agreed to Corpus Juris.

> **From The Manifesto Of The European People's Party**
>
> *Like most parties in the Parliament, the
> EPP supports an integrated Europe.
> The British Conservatives are associates of this party.*
>
> Only the union of Europe can secure its future: a future of freedom and security, progress and solidarity . . .
>
> The EPP will remain watchful that inter-governmental action does not eventually take over from Community action.
>
> The Council procedure of unanimous voting must gradually be restricted . . .
>
> The Commission is the Community's engine . . . The EPP is therefore in favour of the emergence of a genuine European executive power, independent of the Council, which will hold legislative power together with the European Parliament and become a Chamber of States.
>
> The increase in Parliament's powers must not, however, be at the expense of the Commission . . . the Commission must now continue to exercise its right of initiative at every stage of the Parliament-Council legislative process.

All 'recognised' Party groups are funded from the parliamentary budget according to the size of the group.

European parties, with no country link, are likely to become the norm. The Commission has already proposed in the Nice treaty that some MEPs should be elected on European lists. Under Article 191 there will be a new statute for EU political parties, including 'the conditions governing their recognition and the rules regarding their funding.'

The corollary must be that parties which are not 'recognised' will be closed down.

The Democratic Deficit And PR

Voters no longer vote for the man but for the party, which chooses candidates and lists them in order of their importance to the party. Blair's Labour government rapidly embraced the EU method of election, proportional representation: it is a way to divide and rule.

The usual result of a PR election is a compromise: no single party will have a majority and the government becomes a theatre of bartering and horse trading as coalitions form and reform. Under such a system it is easy for a small party, which would otherwise stand no chance in the election, to have power far beyond its numbers.

In the first Scottish Assembly of 1999 Labour did not win an outright majority and chose to share power with the party that came bottom of the polls, the Liberal-Democrats, a travesty of democracy.

In local council elections and European elections any EU citizen can vote. Voting is no longer restricted to citizens of that country. General elections for the British Parliament are still limited to British voters only (though the Irish can now stand as MPs, introduced by the Labour government in 2000) and the first-past-the-post method is still used.

A re-elected Labour government will almost certainly introduce PR for general elections. In that case the British government will be reduced to the lack of authority of an Italian government: little of substance could be achieved.

Meanwhile, the Italians, anxious to abandon PR and adopt the British first-past-the-post system, held a referendum in April 1999 after decades of experience had led to one failed coalition after another and no effective government. Not enough voters turned out to vote: only 49.6 per cent voted and 50 per cent was needed for the result to be valid. Soon they will not have a choice; the EU system will prevail.

Proportional representation

Proportional representation (PR) is an electoral system designed to produce legislative bodies in which the number of seats held by any group or party is proportional to the number of votes cast for members of that group. The power of dominant political parties is reduced and minority groups have a degree of representation previously denied them. Modern systems of PR probably started during the French Revolution. By 1920, almost all the countries of Continental Europe used some form of PR. It was briefly used in some US cities during the early twentieth century.

Of the five PR systems two are used in Britain:
○ Single Transferable Vote or the d'Hondt method (Northern Ireland Assembly, European Parliament)
○ Additional Member System (Scottish Parliament, Welsh Assembly)

Banning Countries, Parties And People

> 'Right-wing populism is one of the major dangers to the European experiment . . .
>
> 'By attacking European integration and its alleged damage to nation states with consequent harm to the sense of nationhood itself – rightwing populism can use a new face of nationalism . . .
>
> 'This new populist nationalism is also displayed in anti-European rhetoric, blaming Brussels for all kinds of economic, political and social problems. The anti-European political discourse pushes aside the benefits and focuses on the costs for society.'
>
> *Discussion paper at the Bern Round Table of the PES, July*
>
> 2000

Every nation has a treason law. So far treason in the EU has not been mentioned but the EU set up a European Monitoring Centre on Racism and Xenophobia in Vienna in 1998. 18 people study 'the evolution of racism, xenophobia and anti-Semitism in the EU, to analyse their causes and consequences.' In the Amsterdam treaty racism and xenophobia were given equal prominence with crime, but only crime was further defined (Article 29, Title VI).

In its work on xenophobia the centre appears to be a watchdog for views opposing the EU,

> 'The centre believes that the legitimacy accorded to the xenophobic views of the Freedom Party [in Austria] by its involvement in government might encourage other xenophobic and anti-Europe parties to try to emulate its campaigning tactics and electoral success. That is why we attach such importance to the charter of European political parties for

The Race Directive

An early product of the EU's Monitoring Centre was a Race Directive. Its promulgation was accelerated because of the controversy sparked by the rise of the Freedom Party in Austria.

The British Commission for Racial Equality will have a new role under the Race Relations Directive. 'Contract compliance', banned by the Conservative government under John Major, will be reintroduced in Britain. Firms will again have to prove that they comply with anti-discrimination law, *before* being awarded a contract. So the burden of proof is reversed in civil race discrimination cases. The onus will be on the accused to prove their innocence once there is a presumption of guilt, eroding a fundamental safeguard in British law.

In June 2000 the Race Directive was voted into British law, even though the Labour government called the code unacceptable just two weeks previously.

a non-racist society, which aims to rid politics of the scourge of xenophobia and the politics of exclusion and fear.'

Dr. Beate Winkler, director, European Monitoring Centre
on Racism and Xenophobia, European Voice, April 2000

The Commission appears to be using a treaty article (Article 7, Title I) to root out 'treason' under which it can cancel a country's voting and other undefined rights but leaving it with all its obligations, including payments to Brussels and enforcing EU laws. A country can be reduced to a colony.

Following a free and democratic election in Austria, Joerg Haider's Freedom Party entered a coalition government with the conservative People's Party in February 2000. In an extreme move, the other 14 EU countries promptly sanctioned Austria.

Britain attacked the incoming Haider coalition: Robin Cook, the Foreign Secretary, told the BBC,

'If we cease our fight against xenophobia and racism, then we put at risk the union that has actually given Europe 50 years of peace.'

3.2.2000

In July 2000 the Austrian Chancellor, Wolfgang Schuessel, set an October deadline for the EU to end sanctions against Austria, pledging that otherwise he would poll Austrians on using 'all suitable means' against the EU. That would have derailed the Treaty of Nice. Immediately the EU appointed three 'wise men' who found a face saving solution, while reporting on Austria's adherence to 'common European values'. Sanctions were duly lifted that September.

The veteran Nazi hunter and Auschwitz survivor, Simon Wiesenthal, attacked the EU's boycott because it was more likely to weaken internal opposition to the Freedom Party than strengthen it. In a joint declaration with the president of the Jewish Community of Austria, Ariel Muzicant, Wiesenthal said,

> 'Austria is a stable and democratic country, which belongs fully to the European family. Racism and persecution are part of its heritage but there is also a long tradition of tolerance and openness.'
>
> *Le Monde, 17.3.2000*

After the Austrian debacle, Jeffrey Titford, a UKIP MEP, asked in the European Parliament if anti-EU parties should be banned. Many MEPs shouted 'Yes'. The Nice treaty will allow that to happen.

In April 2000 the Belgian government, alarmed at the fast growing Flemish nationalist group, Vlaams Blok, recommended a law to 'extinguish the existence of anti-democratic forces'.

The EU's attack on Austria may be just the beginning. The Nice treaty strengthened the provisions of Article 7 under which Austria was sanctioned. It will be even easier for the EU to gang up on one country saying that it is violating the principles of liberty, democracy, respect for human rights and fundamental freedoms and the rule of law. Those principles are open to any interpretation: whose law and whose freedoms?

Until the Nice treaty is ratified, the vote to ban a country has to be unanimous. The new provisions would make it much easier: four fifths of the member states (12) could agree to ban a country so a few allies could not come to its aid.

Furthermore, to attract a ban a country may not have violated the vague EU principles; it may merely pose 'the threat of such a breach'. Again that is open to interpretation.

Under the Nice treaty, Article 191 was strengthened so that the EU sets the rules for EU parties, especially funding, with no national veto.

If countries and perhaps parties can be banned what about newspapers, books, magazines, even television and radio stations? The only evidence to emerge so far that this could be on the cards was in the case of Bernard Connolly, a former head of the EU Commission unit for 'EMS, national and community monetary polices'.

In the European Court of Justice on 19th October 2000 the EU's Advocate-General argued that Connolly's book, *The Rotten Heart Of Europe,* was akin to the publication of a blasphemous work. Since blasphemy could be punished under the European Convention on Human Rights, then a punishment was permissible for offences against 'Europe'. He said that the doctrine of the House of Lords in the case of Derbyshire County Council v. The Times Newspapers (1993) had no foundation in or relevance for European law. The doctrine he rejected on behalf of the EU states that 'It is of the highest public importance that any democratically-elected governmental body, or indeed any governmental body, should be open to uninhibited public criticism.' (Case c-274/99).

A further hint came in October 2000 at a conference on 'Media and Democracy' when the PES, the European Socialist Party (including the British Labour Party), proposed that the EU should create a European Communications Authority. Such an authority could 'recognise' journalists; fund programmes and exert EU control over the media.

The EU Constitution And A Blueprint For Dictatorship?

'There is good reason to accept this text as the basis for an eventual European constitution.'
Gerhard Schroder, German Chancellor, 15.10.2000

After several drafts of documents clearly entitled European

constitutions, the EU agreed in October 2000 on a Charter of Fundamental Rights and Freedoms, which carefully avoided the word constitution.

There are two views on the legitimacy of the Charter. Most of the EU understands that though it is nowhere written that the Charter will form part of the *acquis communitaire* nonetheless the European Court of Justice will take note of it in coming to its decisions. It will be a legal document.

Britain, which successfully argued for riders to be added to many of the rights subjecting them to national laws and customs, believes it is merely aspirational and not legally binding.

France, Germany and the Commission pledged that the Charter was the first draft of an EU Constitution. *Die Welt* (4.10.2000) made clear that it will regulate not only the European institutions, but also 'all national institutions'.

Most of the rights in the Charter are virtually the same as the Convention on European Human Rights or are already part of national constitutions, enforced by national courts.

But this Charter enables the European Court of Justice, on the EU's behalf, to be the guardian of all the EU countries' fundamental rights, removing them from national control.

One article of the Charter indicates that its rights are perhaps not so fundamental. Article 52 (1) states,

> ' . . . limitations [on the exercise of the rights and freedoms recognised by this Charter] may be made only if they are necessary and genuinely meet objectives of general interest being pursued by the Union . . . '

The EU's interest is open to interpretation and the interpreter will be the European Court of Justice. It could be a passport to dictatorship.

The Tentacles Of Brussels: Propaganda

Many thousands of organisations are funded wholly or partly by Brussels and therefore tend to promote the EU's agenda. Among the most important in Britain are,

- Federal Trust, established in 1945, probably one of the
  main means of funding pro-EU groups, publishes semi-
  nal works in favour of the EU and includes among its
  nearly 100 members influential journalists, academics
  and politicians such as Professor Vernon Bogdanor of
  Oxford University, Ian Davidson and Edward Mortimer
  of the *Financial Times*, Peter Riddell of *The Times*,
  Andrew Marr political editor of the BBC, author
  Timothy Garton Ash, Will Hutton, former MEP John
  Stevens and founder of the Pro Euro Conservative Party,
  Charles Kennedy MP, leader of the Liberal Democrats,
  Peter Mandelson MP, Lord Jenkins of Hillhead and
  Baroness Williams
- The European Movement, funded indirectly by the
  Commission and directly by the British government
- Britain in Europe which with the European Movement
  works closely with the Foreign Office to persuade voters
  of the euros' benefits
- The Centre For European Policy Studies, a think tank for
  the EU Commission with a high media profile in Britain
- Jean Monnet professorial chairs at universities, including
  over 1,500 British academics, and students in every
  university in the EU, plus most of the rest of Europe,
  funded wholly or partly by the EU
- Many trade associations, partly EU funded or deliberately set up by the EU to counter 'free' organisations;
  even the British Chambers of Commerce are partly funded by an EU programme, ACTS, run by DG 13

Brussels Manipulates Churches

A Soul For Europe, a Commission project, encourages the integration of Europe using religion for propaganda. According to some estimates *A Soul For Europe* has already given over £25 million ($37.5 million) to pro-EU projects throughout Europe.

Applicants for EU grants must 'explicitly promote the integration of Europe' and 'publicly acknowledge that assistance has been received from the EU'. The scriptures are not mentioned in any *Soul for Europe* literature: this is strictly political.

In 1989 Christianity and the Future of Europe (CAFE) was founded within months of the launch of *A Soul for Europe* and with virtually identical aims. Based in Cambridge and aided by EU grants Canon John Nurser set out 'to construct a multi-lingual, multi-faith Europe with free movement of peoples'.

CAFE influences theological courses at Cambridge University and in theological colleges around Britain to promote the EU. Its successes include a prayer in the new *Common Worship* service book for use in the Church of England,

> 'Eternal God, fount of all authority and wisdom, hear our prayer for those who govern . . . give to the members of the European institutions vision, understanding and integrity, that all may live in peace and happiness, truth and prosperity . . . '

The Vatican Uses Brussels

The Vatican can see advantages in backing the EU. To promote a Europe in which Catholicism might dominate, the

Vatican has pursued EU integration from at least the early 1940s and mainly in secret. The first six members of the EEC were largely Catholic countries. According to John Cornwall's seminal book, *Hitler's Pope, the Secret History of Pius XII*, the Catholic Church today is returning to the ideology of total papal power introduced in the first Vatican Council of 1870. It was this policy which politically disarmed Germany's Catholic community, the most powerful in the world, enabling Hitler to rise to power virtually unopposed. The alliance between the EU and the Papacy could further endanger democracy and accelerate dictatorship.

A Catholic Europe would also end the dominance of Protestantism in Northern Europe. The Vatican is quietly working to overturn the effects of the Reformation over 400 years ago. In Britain that would mean the disestablishment of the Church of England and removing the monarch as head of the Church. In a country where religion is largely a private matter, it may yet set Catholic against Protestant.

The Vatican is already taking a more public stance. The Rome Synod of October 1999 declared it was necessary to,

> 'pursue, with courage and urgency, the process of European integration, widening the circle of member countries of the Union, while appreciating with wisdom the historical and cultural differences of the nations.'

In December 1999 the Vatican began the canonisation process for the so-called 'Founding Fathers of Europe': Konrad Adenauer, Alcide de Gasperi and Robert Schuman.

A Soul For Europe

'The Church of England, individual Anglican Churches and their ministers are actively promoting the dismantling of the United Kingdom and its absorption into the developing European Union super-state. They are doing so with taxpayers' money, channelled through the *Soul for Europe* project, itself part of the little known *Forward Studies Unit* of the European Commission.

'This unit based in Brussels, reports directly to the EU President . . . thus bypassing the supervision of any of the other EU Commissioners. This is due to its strategic importance to the process of European integration . . .

[Set up in 1989, the *Forward Studies Unit*] 'keeps a watching brief on movements in Europe's societies . . . ' [The core of its work is] 'legitimising and constitutionalising the 'European project' . . . applications for funding . . . are filtered through *the Soul for Europe Screening Committee* whose precise membership is secret.'

From English Churchman, a Protestant Family Newspaper,

30.7.1999

Local Voices, 'Communitarisation' By Osmosis

Advisory Community Institutions

The Committee of the Regions
The Economic and Social Committee
Regional Assemblies
Regional Development Agencies

Sharing a lack of power with the European Parliament are two unwieldy and undemocratic groups of 222 people each, the Economic and Social Committee (ECOSOC) and the Committee of the Regions (COR). Both are supposed to represent local people in Brussels. Both are no more than Brussels' wallpaper. ECOSOC was set up by the Treaty of Rome in 1957 and the COR in the 1992 Maastricht Treaty.

ECOSOC entrenches lobby groups in the EU and encourages anyone who wishes to have influence, if influence there be, to form one. The COR gives local authorities, soon to be regional governments, a voice in Brussels, albeit an ineffective one.

They provide a thin gloss of legitimacy to the Commission and act as echo chambers. The Commission wishes to pursue a course of action and these committees provide the calls to action.

They create a new political class in Britain and every other EU country, an inner group to match the new political class in Brussels. Many local officials have reacted enthusiastically to more power and links with other regions in the EU. A few have benefited substantially financially. Not surprisingly they are eager apostles for 'more' EU. It may not occur to them that this also destroys Britain and the nation state.

The Economic and Social Committee
ECOSOC

'It is the body that brings together the socio-occupational interest groups that are the pillars of organised civil society . . . '

ECOSOC represents *stakeholders*.

o Employers: the CBI, the Chambers of Commerce, small businesses
o Workers: mainly from the European Trade Union Confederation
o Other interests: farmers, consumers association, charities and family groups

Its antecedents lie in the 1870/1 Paris communes that under German siege ran Paris according to 'pre-existing social realities'. French federalists have consistently advocated this approach.

Members are nominated by national governments for a renewable four years. Britain with 24 members has been in ECOSOC for over 25 years.

The full group of 222 meets five times a year in Brussels, and 24 members of the inner core or bureau meet eight times a year. They also work in committees. About 135 staff work exclusively for the ECOSOC but it shares another 520 staff with the COR.

ECOSOC delivers about 170 advisory documents and opinions a year.

Committee of the Regions
COR

The EU says the COR 'reflects the opinion' of 85,000 local and regional authorities.

It meets in eight commissions and four sub-committees to comment on EU proposals on town and country planning, energy resources, transport, telecommunications, education and public health.

The British Foreign Office compiles a list of 24 members and 24 alternates every four years. The British delegation is from local authorities, elected or unelected, and balances political party and gender.

The leader of the British delegation is Cllr. Ken Bodfish from Brighton and Hove Council. The party leaders are,

Cllr. Albert Bore, President, PES (Labour)
Cllr. Lord Tope, President, ELDR (Liberal Democrat)
Cllr. Lord Hanningfield of Chelmsford, Vice-President, EPP (Conservative)
Cllr. Milner Whiteman, Vice-President, EA

The EU's Local Government

> 'The government is committed to promoting the development of the English regions, and to devolving decision making down to regional level. It intends to move to directly elected regional government in England, where there is demand for it.'
>
> DETR Annual Report, 1999

In 1997 the new Labour government rapidly embraced the EU's policy of regions, joining the leaders, Spain and Germany. The Commission, intending to eliminate national governments altogether, has divided the 15 countries of the EU into 111 sub-national governments or regions. Britain under the Blair government now has 12 regions. It is hard to avoid the conclusion that Blair wants to end Britain as a country.

EU countries with conservative leaders have been reluctant to espouse regions. President Chirac of France asked the French constitutional court for an opinion (as he also did with minority languages). In 1998 the Portuguese centre-right opposition forced a referendum on the subject.

All regions are described in the same way: 'London in Europe', 'Scotland in Europe', 'Wales in Europe', so abolishing the name of the country but making clear that they are not free and independent.

Each region will have two layers of government: an elected assembly and a development agency with the same boundaries as the European parliamentary constituencies. In Britain, both now exist mainly as appointed bodies.

The first action of most new bodies was to spend taxpayers money on consultants to create a regional identity because none existed. Campaigns, backed with EU money, are calling for more elected Assemblies. Nearly all RDAs have quickly asked for more money and more responsibility. The regional bandwagon is rolling.

Elected Mayors are steadily being introduced, again to fit the EU mould. Their powers and patronage will be vast. The first Mayor of London, Labour's Ken Livingstone, is a twenty-first century baron. He appoints all 15 members of the Transport for London board; 15 members and the chief executive of the London Development Agency; just over half of the new Metropolitan Police Authority, nearly half the new London Fire and Emergency Planning Authority and many other jobs.

Ken Livingstone said,

> 'I've always been pro-Europe. I want to see the end of the nation state, and a united States of Europe so we can stand up to the Americans and the Japanese.'
> *Issue 213, European Information Service interview*

The nineteenth century idea of independent, apolitical civil servants and councils of many equals is fast losing ground. It is likely that corruption will not be far behind.

While the break-up of Britain is certain, the future role of the House of Lords and the House of Commons is as yet obscure. The Lords may become yet another regional assembly with minimal power, partly elected using PR and partly appointed. The House of Commons and with it the British government may fade into obscurity as decisions are taken in Brussels.

The logic of the EU's regional planning suggests that all county councils and parish councils will be abolished. All elected officials will be paid.

The dying old order of local government is trying to embrace the new (see page 280). British County Councils and local authorities have set up offices in Brussels. Several have joined together to defray the expense. The 18 local authorities of Buckinghamshire, Berkshire and Oxfordshire have together set up a Thames Valley office.

British Regional Assemblies or Chambers

Chambers are two-thirds councillors from local authorities and one-third local stakeholders, a mix of ECOSOC and COR at a local level. They number from 40 to over 100 people. Chambers must have a political, gender and ethnic balance.

Chambers first met in 1999. They oversee the Regional Development Agencies (RDAs) to 'provide an over-arching vision for the economic, social and environmental well being of the region'. They prepare regional planning guidance including transport and increase regional ownership. The British government says they will take over the role of the present regional planning bodies.

The eight English regional chambers, not yet elected, are: East Midlands, West Midlands, North-West, North-East Eastern, South-East (SEERA), South West, Yorkshire and Humber Chamber. Each chamber will have a local capital, seat of the elected assembly. In the South-East it will be Winchester, once the capital of England. London will be just one capital among nine in the former England.

Scotland, Wales, Northern Ireland and London were the first elected assemblies in Britain.

> **British Regional Development Agencies**
> **RDAs**
>
> Appointed by the government, the RDAs co-ordinate
> land use, transport, economic development, agriculture,
> energy, and waste, fitting in with EU planning and struc-
> tural funding.
> Eight English RDAs began operation in 1999. All RDAs
> have Brussels offices.
> In 1999 there were more than 160 regional representa-
> tive offices in Brussels.

Euro-Regions

The Commission has invented even larger areas, Euro-
Regions, linking places which have never in recorded history
been united with little in common, or once belonged to a
neighbouring country so deliberately re-opening old wounds.

Examples of Euro-Regions are:

In Britain, East Sussex is linked with Haute-Normandy and
Picardy in France across 70 miles of the English Channel.
Kent is linked with Nord-Pas-de-Calais also across the
English Channel.

In Denmark, the Copenhagen area is joined with Scania in
southern Sweden and linked by a bridge. Scania was Danish
in the seventeenth century.

Germany abuts eight countries and is a prime example of
Euro-regions enveloping neighbouring lands, usually once
claimed by Germany. For example,

- Rhine-Waal includes parts of the Netherlands
- Rhine-Maas is a German speaking area of Belgium with
  part of Germany

○ Southern Jutland in Denmark is linked with Schleswig and Holstein in Northern Germany, a sensitive area that the Germans conquered and annexed from Denmark in 1864

Television and radio broadcast regularly across these borders, funded by the EU to build a new identity, although many locals switch their sets off.

The Outer Border

' . . . incorporation of the Schengen acquis will significantly increase the scope for EU co-operation . . . on such matters as visa and border policies, asylum and immigration, policing, and the exchange of data. All these will impinge directly on the rights of individuals.'

House of Lords Report 'Incorporating the Schengen Acquis into the European Union', 8.9.1998

By 2004 all internal border controls will be abolished and one outer EU border set up. Border policy will be under the total control of Brussels. It will have taken 20 years to achieve. All future members of the EU will immediately have to give up their borders.

1984 – At the Fontainebleau Summit some countries planned to end border controls, 'a pathfinder to an EU-wide frontier free zone.'

1985 – Five countries signed the Schengen Agreement outside the EU treaties and agreed in principle to abolish border controls. They were France, Germany, and the three Benelux countries (Belgium, Luxembourg and the Netherlands). The detail followed in 1990,

○ Abolish systematic checks at borders
○ 'Approximate' visa regulations
○ Strengthen the EU's external border
○ Co-operate on asylum, visa and immigration policy
○ 'Flanking measures' on police and judicial co-operation, and the Schengen Information System (SIS)

> The Schengen Information System is a computer database in Strasbourg, with a section in each country. Immigration authorities, the police and customs and excise can access reports on people wanted for arrest, criminals, missing persons and goods like stolen cars.

1992 – The Maastricht Treaty included border controls, police and judicial co-operation in both civil and criminal matters as 'matters of common interest'. A Committee of senior national officials began work on one policy. For the first time Home Affairs came within the scope of both the European Court of Justice and the Commission but the national veto largely remained.

1997 – The Schengen agreement was brought within the EU as a protocol to the Amsterdam Treaty and a timetable set to remove internal border controls. Britain and Ireland had opt outs. Norway and Iceland, though outside the EU, were included in Schengen, because they had a passport union with Nordic EU counties.

The Old County Councils Seek A New Role
Somerset in Europe

The European Unit . . . plays an active role in European Organisations:

o Atlantic Arc
o Assembly of European Regions
o Close liaison with the Committee of the Regions
o Lobbies for Somerset with the European Parliament, MEPs, the European Commission, its Directorates and the Local government International Bureau (the UK representation in Europe for Local Authorities)
o Wins European funding
o The Somerset Twinning Co-ordinator helps Somerset communities already twinned with towns and villages across Europe and encourages new twinning links

From Somerset County Council web site,
www.somerset.gov.uk

The European Border Police

' . . . the costs of delaying enlargement would greatly exceed the costs of carrying it through on time.
The clear prospect of future accession dictates the
pace and scope of reforms in the acceding countries.
Without it, stability in these countries, and very
soon in their Western neighbours – especially
Germany – would be jeopardised.'

> Dr. Wolfgang Schäuble and Karl Lamers,
> CDU/CSU paper, 1998

From early 2001 the German and Italian governments will
exchange border troops as the vanguard of an EU force to
secure the EU's outer frontiers after the next wave of enlargement.

Given the political sensitivities about stationing German
border guards on Polish soil, Berlin has promoted a joint EU
force in which every country would participate on equal
terms. The Germans were concerned that weak security along
their eastern borders had led to a surge of illegal immigration
and increased crime.

The European border police will protect the borders of
new member states like Poland, the Czech Republic and
Slovakia to the east. In March 2000 Germany proposed that
the EU should help to police the 3,000 km of Polish border,
nearly half of which borders Russia, Belarus and Ukraine.
And at Germany's behest a border fence was built on Poland's
eastern border to block illegal immigrants and smuggling.
Because it also prevents normal trade in a poor part of the
country it is having a costly effect on Poles.

10,000 of Germany's 40,000 Federal Border Guards may
join the EU border patrol, as the German frontiers with
Poland and the Czech Republic are removed under the
Schengen system.

People On The March

Since the fall of the Berlin Wall in 1989 about four million migrants have entered Europe. Because of the Schengen agreement they can now roam freely around most of the EU countries.

More than 400,000 immigrants arrived in Britain in 1998 alone, one of the highest numbers on record. Most come from other EU countries now able to work in Britain without restriction under the open borders' policy. About a quarter seek asylum. On top of that, there is an unknown but presumably large number of illegal immigrants.

Professor James Walvin of York University said, 'This is as large a movement of people as we have had for a very long time, if ever. I think you would be hard-pressed to match these figures with anything in history. It could be a unique figure even by comparison with the post World War One years when the whole of Europe was on the move.'

Other comparable times of high immigration were the Irish potato famine in the 1840s and the arrival of thousands of immigrants from the Caribbean 50 years ago.

Partly from a Daily Telegraph report, 1.12.1999

The British Opt Out Only To Opt In

The Labour government has kept Britain's borders and visa and asylum controls but has given way to the EU where it believes there is advantage to be had.

In 1999 Britain agreed to opt into part of Schengen on,

- ○ Police co-operation
- ○ Mutual assistance in criminal matters
- ○ Narcotic drugs
- ○ Schengen Information System
- ○ Data protection

The Commission believes Britain's opt out, or what remains of it, will become unsustainable and, in the medium term, Britain will sign up to Schengen in full and its borders will cease to exist.

All Europe Will Be EU

One of the cleverest pieces of EU propaganda is the use of the word 'Europe' to describe the EU. But it is more than propaganda. Unsung, the Council of Europe of 41 countries and the EU of 15 are working together to achieve total integration, even from Vladivostok to the Atlantic. The Council of Europe was once intended to be the EU of today but a British Prime Minister, Clement Attlee, sidelined the project and for several decades it remained nothing more than a talking shop, until the tempo of EU integration increased in the early 1980s.

Today, the Council of Europe is known as 'the waiting room' for the EU and has already expanded its membership into Eastern Europe and into the former USSR (Russia is a member). Because it is seen as a talking shop, countries and regions are ensnared into the EU project without realising that the end aim is to take them over.

While the EU is outlawing most national differences, from Imperial weights and measures, to currencies and legal systems, it is promoting, even creating other local differences and at great cost. This can only be part of its deliberate policy to divide and rule.

The three organisations below, under the Council of Europe banner, help that process. Many hundreds of people are directly employed by them, and many thousands more attend regular conferences and committee meetings.

Europe Wide Integration

1951 – The Council of European Municipalities and Regions

1973 – The Conference of Peripheral Maritime Regions

1985 – The Assembly of European Regions

After the Second World War Germany advocated town twinning with France. French and German mayors founded the Council of European Municipalities and Regions (CEMR) in 1951. It promotes regions and towns to 'make them sufficiently strong and able to deal with their central state . . . [to] fight for the political union of Europe.' Twinning is a political act with cultural overtones. The Commission (DG X) partly funds it.

Over 13,000 European towns have been twinned under the CEMR's charter. A guide, *The Directory of European Twinnings,* helps participants.

The Golden Stars award is presented annually to twinned towns which have 'best contributed to European integration'.

The more towns, the greater the distance and the more languages in each twinning project, the better the chance of winning.

The Town Twinning Oath

The Mayors: On this day, we take a solemn oath to maintain permanent ties between our municipalities, to encourage exchanges in all domains between their inhabitants so as to develop, through a better mutual understanding, the notion of European brotherhood, to join forces so as to further, to the best of our ability, the success of this vital enterprise of peace and prosperity: THE UNION OF EUROPE.

The CEMR promotes a *Citizens Europe* for the whole continent with over 100,000 local and regional authorities led by the former French President, Giscard D'Estaing. British representatives are from the Local Government Association led by Councillor Ken Bodfish.

The CEMR has sponsored another five charters including *The European Charter of Local Self-government* of 1985 which encourages local authorities 'to form consortia with other local authorities . . . to carry out tasks of common interest.' The Labour government signed the Charter soon after assuming office in 1997.

A Tower of Babel

English is the world's leading language and is spoken by half of the EU, yet the signatory countries to *The Charter of Minority Languages* of 1992 agreed to promote regional or minority languages. Britain signed almost straight away.

The Charter of Minority Languages

The Charter ensures, encourages or provides for the use of the minority language in,

- Links between all minority language groups
- Education from pre-school to university, adult courses and teacher training
- In libraries, museums, archives, theatres, cinemas, and festivals at home and abroad
- Judicial proceedings wholly or in part
- In documents and debates
- Place names and family names
- Translation services, dubbing and subtitling for administrative, commercial, economic, social, technical or legal terminology
- Recruiting and training officials and appointing public employees with a knowledge of the language
- At least one radio station, TV channel, newspaper or encourage programmes and newspaper articles
- Funds for the media to use the language and train journalists
- Guarantees not to block the retransmission of radio and TV broadcasts from neighbouring countries in the language
- No discrimination against the language e.g. in employment contracts and product instructions and promote it in all public places e.g. banks, hospitals, hostels and in safety instructions
- A body to monitor progress and report every three years to the Council of Europe

Across Europe there are over 100 minority languages, usually around national borders, reflecting Europe's chequered past over thousands of years, and many of them had virtually died out between 1000 and 1600. In a bizarre move to reverse the historical trend, within one generation and with EU money and organisation much of local life may once again be carried out in these languages.

Insistence on the use of minority languages, especially in education, will ensure that the locality is isolated and limit the opportunities for people in the wider world. It will make them second class citizens and easier to control. All regional assemblies will have translation services, which will further reduce their effectiveness.

In Britain, Cornish, Gaelic, Irish, Scots, Welsh, and Manx are being revived and even the Guernsey patois with a plan to import French teachers. In Northern Ireland three languages are promoted: English, Gaelic and Scots. Wales is the most advanced with extensive schooling in Welsh.

Germany, the prime mover for minority languages, founded the European Centre for Minority Issues based in Flensburg in 1996 with Denmark and Schleswig-Holstein, the area it conquered over 100 years ago. The centre promotes,

> 'universal, regional, bilateral and national standards that may assist in consolidating democratic governance on the basis of ethnic diversity and human rights.'

It is of great significance that the Nice treaty allows a country to be overruled on any aspect of its treatment and relationship with any minority group within its borders. Brussels is acquiring the right to interfere in nation states to promote regionalism.

The issue is even more acute on the continent. Italy has 11 minority languages, and the small country of Belgium four.

A Cornish Revival

'The Cornish language is supposed to have died out in about 1800 . . . One might ask the extent to which the language is now spoken. The night before last, I was judging the finals of the Pan-Celtic Song for Cornwall competition on local radio. There were 32 entries – all sung in the Cornish language . . . it is estimated there are approximately 3,000 Cornish speakers . . .

'Cornwall County Council has established a policy to support the language . . . being specified within the European Charter for Regional or Minority Languages. There are at least three regular periodicals solely in the language – *An Gannas, An Gowser* and *An Garrick*. The two local radio stations, Radio Cornwall and Pirate FM, have regular news broadcast . . . and other programmes and features for learners and enthusiasts.

'Local newspapers such as the *Western Morning News* have regular articles in Cornish.'

Andrew George, MP for St Ives, House of Commons, 23.2.1999

Germany has at least 17. President Chirac of France, where there are eight border languages, took the issue to the French Constitutional Council in July 1999, which ruled that the Charter on Minority and Regional Languages was incompatible with the French constitution.

The EU's 11 official languages, which already cause confusion and huge expense in Brussels, will become over 50. On enlargement the number will shoot up again. Germany is already strongly promoting German to be the EU official language.

Isles Language Festival

Communities in the Western Isles will welcome more than 300 youngsters and their leaders from 14 minority language regions throughout Europe this month. The festival of lesser-used languages, for 10 to 12 year-olds, is being held for the first time in the Western Isles . . .

Groups from Denmark, Eire, France, Germany, Holland, Italy, Sweden, Wales, and for the first time Northern Ireland, will be participating in a programme of sporting and cultural activities and local tours. Pupils from Uist and Barra will be representing the Gaelic community in Scotland.

The Herald, 5.4.1999

The Conference Of Peripheral Maritime Regions (CPMR)

'The object of the CPMR over the next 20 to 30 years is to make the maritime Regions the gateways of a new continent under construction.'

126 maritime regions are in the CPMR, based in Rennes,

Brittany and are part of the EU planning system. In 1985 the CPMR created an Assembly of European Regions (AER) which works with the European Parliament, the Committee of the Regions, and the Economic and Social Committee. Many of the representatives are the same.

The five commissions are,

Atlantic Arc	29 regions	5 countries
Mediterranean	42 regions	7 countries
North Sea	22 regions	4 countries
Baltic	25 regions	7 countries
Islands	25 regions	11 countries

There are special groups, for example on fisheries.

European Planning

The EU has long recognised the importance of planning rules and regulations for 'collectivist' command. The EU partly funds many projects which are nearly all cross-border.

Each project costs the taxpayer about twice as much as it would if funded nationally. For every two pounds paid to the EU, Brussels keeps one and gives one to the project, which it controls. The national government, with no control over the project, has to match funds pound for pound and also provide the working capital because the EU will only pay at the end.

Since 1994 the EU has been planning across the whole of Europe helped by organisations like the Conference of Peripheral Maritime Regions. The EU has no authority to carry out planning on this scale, it is voluntary, but there has been no national resistance to EU funding. Called the European Spatial Development Plan, it aims 'to achieve the gradual economic integration of Europe, the growing role of regional and local authorities.' It develops,

o EU border regions and their cities including gateway cities
o Euro-corridors
o Strategies for clusters of towns and cities in cross-border areas
o Transport and telecommunications (encouraging less car use by road pricing and energy taxes)
o Technology, business, industry and agriculture
o Education, culture and tourism
o Natural assets including water resources
o Risk management for natural disasters
o Housing

This vast plan fits inside an even bigger plan for the whole continent overseen by the Council of Europe, called CEMAT or 'the guiding principles for sustainable spatial development of the European Continent countries.'

The EU also runs and partly funds five-year plans, which began in 1990, 'to accelerate the integration of internal border areas into a single internal market and to reduce the isolation of external border areas.'

They are all cross-border projects, for example linking the East Coast of Ireland with North Wales. No part of the EU has escaped. The 1995 to 1999 phase cost £1.9 billion ($2.8 billion). An energy plan, Regens, links countries by electricity cable and gas pipelines so they become interdependent and no longer self-sufficient. The latest plan cost £500 million ($750 million) over 5 years.

Two huge projects illustrate the EU's designs,

o North-western Metropolitan Area with nearly half the EU's population covers Belgium, Denmark, France, Ireland, Luxembourg, Netherlands, and Britain with a plan 'to act as a testing ground for new policy ideas and a seedbed for development strategy'

○ Vision and strategies around the Baltic 2010 (VASAB 2010) integrates 'countries in the *greater European space*.' It includes EU countries (Finland, Sweden, Denmark, Germany) and Russia, Estonia, Latvia, Lithuania, Belarus, Poland and Norway

Under the Nice treaty, Brussels' control will tighten: the national veto will end for,

○ Town and country planning, the management of the quantitative aspects of water resources
○ Land use with the exception of waste management
○ Energy sources a country may use and the structure of its energy supply

Enlargement To The East And South-East

'The enlargement we are talking about is not just any enlargement, but rather a decisive step towards the unification of the continent, a change in nature and scale.'

Pierre Moscovici, Minister Delegate for European Affairs, to students of the École Polytechnique, Palaiseau,

31.1.2000

For security and for profit Germany wants to control the countries to its east and south-east, its traditional areas of interest. The German answer is to absorb those countries into the EU. It was therefore critical for a German to hold both posts of Commissioner for Enlargement and the key post in the Balkans.

Whether deliberately or not, a new German-led Empire will arise. Britain, always a global trading country facing the Atlantic is now finding that despite its own economic interests it has to back German expansion in the east.

Karl Lamers and Dr. Wolfgang Schäuble wrote in their 1994 CDU/CSU Paper, *Reflections on European Politics,*

> 'If European integration were not to progress, Germany might be called upon, or be tempted by its own security constraints, to try to effect the stabilisation of Eastern Europe on its own and in the traditional manner.'

The German phrase for 'traditional manner' clearly meant by armed force.

Who is in the EU's waiting room?

Near the way in: Hungary, Poland, the Czech Republic, Slovenia, Estonia and Cyprus.

Next in line: Bulgaria, Latvia, Lithuania, Malta, Romania and Slovakia.

Uncertain: Turkey has to meet EU standards on democracy and human rights, notably in its relations with the Kurds and with Greece on the subject of Cyprus. The US backs Turkey's entry.

Deepening First

Whenever the EU has increased its membership, it has deliberately increased its central powers, 'deepening in order to widen'. Under the Nice Treaty major adjustments had to be made to include as many as 28 members, almost doubling the existing number.

Institutional reforms include,

o Increasing the number of Commissioners from 20 on the

basis of one per country. Britain, Germany, France, Spain and Italy will lose one of their two Commissioners from 2005

○ Increasing the power of the EU President to direct the Commission's policy with more authority over the other Commissioners on casting votes and the allocation of portfolios

○ New Vice-Presidents increasing their number to 6 or 8, to co-ordinate the Commission's activities in given areas

○ The President to assign special tasks or responsibilities to Commissioners without portfolio

○ Re-weighting the votes of each Member State, an extra 5 votes to those countries giving up one of their two Commissioners

The likely date for the next enlargement is 2006 because,

○ France and Germany have agreed to stage another inter-governmental conference in 2004 to 'reshape' the EU institutions. Differences remain on how many countries will be admitted in 2006

○ By then the special EU aid payments to the poorer nations of Spain, Portugal, Ireland and Greece will have stopped, allowing more money to be given to the new entrants

○ The German government, likely to bear a large part of the cost of expansion and worried about migration from the east, is anxious to avoid enlargement becoming an issue in its 2002 general election

○ Bankers are concerned about rushing the admission of new members into the EU and immediately into the euro. The euro's falling exchange rate was partly affected by market concerns on EU enlargement increasing risk and cost

Subsidies and security are the principal reasons why countries wish to join the EU. The Commissioner for Enlargement, the German Gunther Verheughen, publishes 'progress reports' on the economic 'reform' being carried out by candidate countries, which include huge restructuring and mass layoffs.

The longer entry is postponed the more difficult it will be to win popular support. Poland, Hungary and the Czech Republic had been expecting entry to the EU by 2003. In Poland, opposition to EU membership is growing and as many as half the Poles are against. Poland and Brussels have been at loggerheads over agriculture. Poland tried to protect its agriculture from destruction by the EU's practice of dumping heavily subsidised agricultural products. In 1999 the Poles presented the EU with a list of about 400 products on which import duties were to be increased by as much as five times. These tariffs were to kick in when the volume of imports rose above a certain level.

Expansion To The Balkans

Germany has the dominant interest in expanding the EU into the Balkans and has been in the forefront of all international activity in the trouble spots of the Balkans, such as Bosnia and Kosovo.

The German Presidency of the EU promoted a Stability Pact with the long-term goal admitting five Balkan states – Albania, Croatia, Bosnia-Herzegovina, Macedonia and Yugoslavia – into the EU and meanwhile offering them associate membership. NATO membership was also offered as a long-term goal. The Stability Pact for South Eastern Europe was agreed in June 1999. It reads like an abridged Treaty of Rome.

The Pact included all the Balkan countries plus the EU, US, Canada and Japan and many international organisations to run the Balkans. It is a bureaucratic nightmare.

EU Ministers approved £170 million ($255 million) in special aid for the refugee crisis, and nearly half went directly to Montenegro, Albania and Macedonia. Since 1991 the EU has allocated over £5 billion ($7.5 billion). For 2002 to 2006, the EU plans to spend a further £6.7 billion ($10.5 billion).

Led by France and Germany, in April 1999 the ECOFIN Council of Finance Ministers, agreed to grant a debt moratorium of some £100 million ($150 million) to the countries bordering Kosovo. The German Finance Minister presented the plan as part of an overall German project to create what he called a Marshall Plan for the Balkans.

To achieve this aim, Chancellor Schroder announced that Bodo Hombach, Minister in the Chancellor's Office and one of the most powerful politicians in Germany, was appointed as the EU's Co-ordinator for the Stability Pact, and was responsible for administering the reconstruction funds.

German industry could only benefit. According to a *Handelsblatt* report (25.6.1999) the president of the German Federation of Industry telephoned Hombach to say that his appointment to the Balkans was 'in the vital interest of German industry.' Germany has a strong interest in the oil and gas pipelines, which may now be built across the Balkans to transport fuel from the Caspian Sea.

The EU is masterminding another ambitious project linking Greece with the rest of the EU, the Adriatic-Ionian highway. The 745 mile (1,200 kilometres) motorway will run from Trieste in Italy to Igumenice in Greece, along the coastline of Slovenia, Croatia, Bosnia, Montenegro and Albania. Construction may begin by 2003. Soft loans will be available from the European Investment Bank for this multi-billion dollar project.

The End Within One Decade

The EU's superstructure is already in place. Enlargement to the east is on track for 2006. A wider web has been spun over the whole of Europe using the Council of Europe and the Stability Pact for the Balkans. The divide and rule policy, actively pursued for years, is accelerating. Strong national governments are being replaced with weak, ineffective regional assemblies speaking a multitude of languages and reporting directly to Brussels. The EU inner core, led by Germany and France, is strengthening and via the Treaty of Nice will have the power to advance to one country by 2010.

The United States of Europe will have arrived.

Chapter 13

THE END OF THE BEGINNING AND
THE BEGINNING OF THE END

It has become clear with the passage of time that Britain made a bad bargain in signing the Treaty of Rome and its subsequent amendments.

Britain has given up much of its independence to a highly centralised state, led by Germany and France, with interests far removed from British interests. The British people are paying a very high price for no benefits.

For the first 50 years the EU has primarily been concerned with matters economic. Today the EU is poised to take control of criminal justice, the police, and the armed forces. No freedoms as the British understand them will be left. Soon, both freedom of speech and of action will begin to be curtailed. Democracy will be dead.

This is not a local affair, limited to Europe. The EU, an inflexible power bloc, is bent on challenging the US, which it sees as a rival on the world stage. That could endanger the whole world. The EU espouses none of the freedoms that the US, Britain or the Commonwealth hold dear. The EU sees its future as challenging and overtaking the US for global superiority.

The British government under Tony Blair has made few moves to withstand the constant attack on Britain's remaining freedoms. In many areas such as breaking up the United Kingdom into EU regions, voting systems, foreign policy, the armed forces, the defence industry and the criminal justice system, the Labour government has warmly embraced the

Brussels' bear. The British government has constantly denied that it is working against British interests but its actions speak louder than words. It is the final betrayal.

Britain should stand fast for its independence, withdraw from the EU and negotiate advantageous trading agreements based on mutual economic interest.

Because the EU is increasingly manifesting protectionism, it may not be possible to reach a satisfactory arrangement with the EU.

Nevertheless the trading and economic opportunities in the modern word are endless and limitless. Many people of good faith on both sides of the Atlantic have suggested that Britain's future lies in closer economic relationships with North America.

Britain can encourage and expand its trade with the Commonwealth. Many Commonwealth countries, especially those round the Pacific, have a potential that will easily eclipse the statist European Union.

Above all Britain should not abandon its freedoms, traditions and democracy that have made the country one of the leading nations of the world.

Britain Held Hostage
The Coming Euro-Dictatorship

Lindsay Jenkins

'The prognosis for all our future'
Frederick Forsyth

Lindsay Jenkins

Britain Held Hostage

With a dramatic new foreword by
Frederick Forsyth

ISBN 0-9657812-1-6

Britain Held Hostage, The Coming Euro-Dictatorship revealed for the first time who created the European Union and why. Even before the Second World War British and American friends in high places planned one Europe, Wartime resistance leaders fought for a superstate with no Hitler, but it took the Americans to make it happen.

Today Britain has a new constitution, the Treaty of Rome; British law is subservient to European law. Shortly Britain may be a province in a German-led Europe. Proposals for one army and one police force are only the latest in a long line of 'small steps' leading to 'major consequences' for British voters. Soon the British will know they won the war but lost the peace.

Available from
The June Press, PO Box 9984, London W12 8WZ
Telephone/Fax 44+(0)20-8746 1206
www.junepress.com

An Orange State Press Book
Washington, DC
www.orangestatepress.com